GW01451787

BEXLEY PUBS

The History of your Local

by

James Packer

London Borough of Bexley
Libraries & Museums Department
1995

Published 1995

British Library Cataloguing in Publication Data.
A catalogue record for this book is available
from the British Library

© 1995. J. E. Packer

Bexley Libraries & Museums

Hall Place, Bourne Road, Bexley, Kent DA5 1PQ

ISBN 0 902541 33 1
Designed by Bexley London Borough Graphic Studio

Bexley
LONDON BOROUGH

*No part of this publication may be reproduced, stored in a retrieval system or
transmitted in any form or by any means, electronic, mechanical, photocopying,
recording or otherwise, without prior permission of the Chief Librarian*

*T*o

Joe Packer   &   Joey Packer
(1903 - 1962)   (1941 - 1956)

for pints together missed

& to

my very good friend

Mick Fielder

(1934 - keep ticking)

for pints together enjoyed

Jim Packer

(1947 - keep drinking)

Contents

Preface

*P*ubs, sometimes fuelled by their merchandise can encourage strong opinions. These may variously concern the relative merits of establishment and the goods, services and entertainments available. Other imbibers may reflect on the currently changing nature of this celebrated aspect of British culture and how pubs have evolved over time. Pubs have come and gone with the fortunes of towns, at the behest of the brewery or the quality of the management. Despite this (and along with the church) they are an enduring feature of our townscape, and although the two institutions have apparently opposite purposes both are key to the social fabric of a community, acting as meeting place, a diversion and relief from work and domestic routine and a place that offers support to those in need.

This small book tells for the first time the story of all pubs currently in the London Borough of Bexley. Where established the founder and foundation dates for each pub and building are given and rebuilding and major alterations and changes in ownership are recorded. Notable, unusual, humorous and sometimes macabre events in a pub's history are also recounted. This is all set in the context of the changing scene, nationally and locally. Each pub has an illustration, many of which have never been published before.

I hope it will promote discussion and interest in the subject. It may settle or inflame disputes over pub history or confirm or undermine claims of association with the famous or infamous.

It is the product of many years enthusiastic and meticulous research using a huge range of sources in almost as wide a variety of locations. Like its subject it is intended to bring pleasure, but it is principally a tribute to a vital part of Bexley's heritage.

Len Reilly
Bexley Local Studies Librarian
December 1994

Introduction

I have been interested in history in general since primary school days. Later, a keener interest developed in my local history. Pubs have always fascinated me, possibly it's something in the blood - my mother briefly working behind the bar and my father the other side, enjoying a pint (or two).

An article in a local newspaper a few years ago stating that there were 100 pubs in the London Borough of Bexley, of which (then) only one, the White Swan, was a freehouse, set me on a course which has resulted in this initial offering.

After sitting in the office trying to list as many pubs as my colleague Terry Williams and I could remember - about eighty-seven - we resorted to the phone directory for the balance. Then naturally followed the question of how many of them I had sampled - about seventy-eight. The next task was having a drink in the remaining pubs, usually undertaken with my good friend Mick Fielder after we had attended the monthly meetings of the Erith & Belvedere Local History Society. This is called 'field' research, otherwise known as a good excuse for a pint.

Then came the harder academic research, an exciting quest over the years mainly through primary records. These sources and their limitations are discussed in Appendix I and II.

The origins of many local pubs go back to a relaxation in the law in 1830. Prior to that date the licensing of pubs for the sale of alcoholic drinks annually came under the watchful eye of magistrates at special 'brewster sessions'. There were thirty-seven pubs by the time of the 1830 Beerhouse Act. This Act was introduced partly as an aid to combat a (diminishing) gin drinking problem and as part of the free trade movement. It allowed any householder whose name was on the rate book to obtain a licence from the Excise Authorities on payment of two guineas (£2.10p) for the sale of beer, ale, porter, cider and perry.

Like the rest of the country this had an immediate effect locally. Allowing for the vagaries in surviving records it appears that within two years the number of pubs had jumped to fifty-eight, an increase of over 55%. By 1845, even allowing for the closure of some short lived experimental ventures, numbers had doubled. Numbers trading were almost three and a half times those of 1830 when they peaked in 1869. Growth to 1832 was mainly in Bexley Parish but whereas the village stabilised after this initial spurt Bexley New Town or Bexleyheath as it was becoming called, saw a constant increase to 1869. For Crayford village and Erith town their large increases occurred in the ten years to 1869. This was the year that beerhouses were brought back under the control of magistrates and unsatisfactorily conducted houses were closed down. More went after the 1904 Act which paid compensation for pubs declared 'redundant' due to high densities and of a low volume of trade.

Railways were the great wonder of the Victorian age, opening up much land to commerce and commuters. Publicans soon capitalised on this since the type of person using the railway were conceived somehow to be of a better class or at least prefer drinks which had a better profit margin. Pubs were renamed and those newly built tried to obtain spirit licences on the basis that they should be regarded as the privileged 'Railway Hotel'.

There was a pub property speculation boom in the 1890's which in our area created about a dozen new or rebuilt pubs. In the 1920's and 1930's our district saw the waves of estate building rolling across our agrarian heritage. Almost two dozen pubs were built or rebuilt in this period. Such was the increase in a thirsty population that rebuilt pubs like the Blue Anchor, Bridgen and the Woodman, Blackfen were further extended in these years.

I have tried to make this book more than just a catalogue of dates though I am extremely interested when pubs came into being and why at a certain location. I was never particularly interested in when pubs changed from the status of beerhouse to having a full on licence also retailing spirits. To me a pub is a social meeting place and a community asset. Repeated mention of applications at the annual licensing sessions have been brought in for the light they shine on various aspects of local history, which I trust will prove of interest. I have tried to include aspects of changes in licensing law mainly culled from reports of when landlords accidentally or otherwise infringed them.

The derivation of unusual or specifically local pub signs is given where known but many require no explanation as they are either culled from the general gamut of popular, familiar sounding names or heraldry. Any previous name for a pub is separated from the current one by a '/' and any nickname is in brackets.

Hence 'Royal Oak (Polly Clean Stairs)/Woodman' indicates that the Royal Oak is nicknamed the Polly Clean Stairs and was once the Woodman. Also I have included notes about previous internal arrangements of bars, this I feel being of especial interest to you looking around your local and hopefully explaining some of those odd shapes, corners and mysteriously placed RSJ's.

I have only written about pubs existing today, those that are no longer with us are excluded since I intend them to form the subject of a further volume. Old pubs which called themselves 'Hotel' on the basis of sometimes less than half a dozen rooms are included. Modern restaurants with bars are excluded since the latter are ancillary to the main function although today with the building of dining extensions onto old established pubs the distinction is getting blurred.

This work is not a good (or bad) pub guide. There are some locals I would not consider trying again, except perhaps after a few years. Similarly the type I like, you may hate. What is good is that out there is an institution, part of our heritage, dedicated to pleasing the imbibers of our Borough. So publicans, I raise my tankard to you - long may your history continue!

Acknowledgements

Acknowledgements are due firstly to all present and past members of Bexley Local Studies Centre, Hall Place who have patiently helped me in my enquiries. Particular thanks to Malcolm Barr-Hamilton, Local Studies Officer, who through his wide knowledge of his collections produced relevant items that had been secreted away. Especial thanks are due to Local Studies Librarian, Len Reilly, who persuaded me to set some of my researches down on paper and then, when I wrote more than even I thought possible, had the unenviable task of suggesting ways of condensing it into a manageable size. Frances Sweeny carried out the task of retyping the text. The book was designed at short notice by Bexley's Graphics Studio.

Also to the County Record Office, Maidstone, for deeds and wills and more importantly the records of licensed victuallers (1646-1827) and for the lead weights to prevent the untimely rewrapping of those six foot long vellum licensing rolls. Thanks for the courtesy and time shown by Ken Thomas, Archivist for Courages (FBG Holdings Ltd) and George Caton of Charringtons. To the Greater London Record Office for access to documents from Trumans and some constituent parts of the Courage empire. To our neighbours, Greenwich Local History Library, for the records of 18th century Blackheath Petty Sessions.

To Dartford Reference Library for access to the Dartford Chronicle from 1869, a vital four years before the first surviving Bexley newspapers. To Martyn Nicholls, Senior Planning Officer for the London Borough of Bexley (and local CAMRA Secretary) for assistance from his own busy time for dates of post 1918, new and rebuilt pubs which until the writing of this book I had not studied in depth.

I should like to thank the following individuals for granting permission to reproduce their illustrations:

Mrs D E Wethered, neé Livett 9

Museum of London 10, 11

Courage archives 26, 33

Mr Mount 32, 38l, 38r, 55r, 56r, 62

Mick Fielder 34r, 37, 48, 64

The John Topham Picture Library
. . . . .35r, 65, 70, 72r

H. C. Davies 55l

Mr A C Cunningham 74r

Centre for Kentish Studies 75l

Author 15l, 25r, 49l, 56l, 68r,
75r, back cover

All remaining illustrations are part of the Bexley Local Studies Collection.

Had I been a dog owner I would at this point have thanked faithful Rover for having guided his master safely home after occasions of too much research at one of our local establishments; however I made it on my own.   To Messrs N Call, T Cobley et al for all their valuable help.

And finally to local publicans for providing liquid inspiration over the years.

Bexley

Black Horse - Albert Road

*I*n the 1850s the area around Albert Road and Hartford Roads was known as the Building Fields and later as Upper Webbs Field. The pub was built in 1859 by Vincent Brown a well digger who by the following year had built four cottages nearby. This was another venture into

The Black Horse, 1951.

beer retailing as he had already opened a beer house in Vicarage Road. The Albert Road establishment was a success and no doubt caused the demise of another nearby beerhouse in Bourne Road.

His widow ran it from the mid-1860's and leased it to Kidd, the Dartford brewer, from 1876. She left the pub in her will to William King (of the Hare & Hounds) for his lifetime and afterwards jointly to those of his children who reached the age of twenty-one. Six did so, and Kidds had to buy its freehold in piece-meal stages between 1889 and 1904.

In Edwardian times the pub had a separate private bar to the left of the door with a large club room behind this, a small public bar centre left and on the right a tap room as big as the two other bars together. Until recently there lay a private living room behind the tap for the proprietor's use.

Black Prince - Bourne Road

*C*harringtons started applying for a licence for a new pub, next to the recently built Rochester Way, in 1929. This was not granted until 1934 when work commenced to build a classic road house on the site of Bourne Place, a large substantially Victorian house demolished in 1933. The original name they planned for it was the Robin Hood but this was dropped, probably because of the similarly named pub in Bexleyheath. The chosen name is meant to reflect an association between the Black

The Black Prince, 1951.

Prince, this part of Kent and (inaccurately) nearby Hall Place. The brewers anticipated spending some £14,000 and it was to have a dining room capable of seating 120. It opened on the 27th September 1935 and was greatly enlarged in 1981 by Crest Hotels.

Coach & Horses - North Cray Road

*T*his is first mentioned by name in 1793 run by Thomas Long who had held a licence since 1769. It may be as early as 1762. A building originally of three bays, it had an unusual

A bill head for the Coach and Horses, 1847.

The Coach and Horses, 1951

entrance in that the doors were a few feet off the ground. It was claimed to be so designed to enable passengers to walk straight out of their coach into the hostelry.

Beasleys of Plumstead seem to have acquired it in 1875 when Robert Nelson Stratton, a fruiterer of Bexleyheath, became licensee. It became an Ind Coope house in 1978.

In 1905 the local Police Inspector reported to the licensing magistrates that an Air-Gun Club met in the tap room and had in fact a shooting gallery there. To laughter in the licensing court, attention was drawn to the fact that the police had 'personal experience' of the range. The appeal by the publican that they had a certificate of the National Air Rifle Association, under the patronage of no less a figure than Lord Roberts (hero of the Boer War) was dismissed on the grounds that the said Lord did not licence Public Houses! The licensee, Thomas Radcliffe, was a retired quartermaster sergeant and gave evidence that over a 1000 clubs were on licensed premises. The Police Inspector noted that anyone who went in could obtain ammunition ('ten slugs a penny') and use the range. The magistrates were told that the tap room was put out of bounds to the general public when shooting commenced. The magistrates thought it was still too dangerous a practice and Radcliffe was compelled to close it down.

George - High Street

The George is first mentioned in licensing records in 1713. It was leased for part of the 18th century by Taskers Brewery of Dartford, and was from the 1820's under various partnerships of Lewisham brewers Stewart, Marsden and Nicholls until 1891 when Whitbreads took over. It was rebuilt in 1878 and over subsequent years the bars expanded into the covered driveway from the High Street

premises. The first known licence for this site was held by Robert Dickenson between 1713 and 1723. He also held a licence for The Three Kings in 1705 which is possibly the same building. It was purchased in 1757 by John Pettet, a Dartford brewer, and remained a tied house until 1993.

The low extension on the front is a late Victorian addition and the restaurant section is modern. The pub suffered a fire in April 1972 which did some damage to the early part of the building.

The George showing the drive into the rear yard, c.1915.

to the rear yard. A public campaign recently encouraged the owners to retain the old established name in addition to the newer, fancier 'Hogshead Alehouse'.

Kings Head - High Street

This is one of the oldest buildings in the village and is amongst its oldest established pubs. A Kings Head is mentioned in the 1681 survey of the Manor of Bexley but it is not these

Millers Arms/Hare & Hounds - High Street

Beer is first known to have been sold here in 1855 when Henry King is listed in a trade directory as a beer retailer. He may be the same (or the son of the) Henry King who moved to the site in 1831 from the George across the road. He is known to have been a baker but there is no evidence of him trading as a beer retailer in the intervening period. The pub appears to have changed its name from the Hare and Hounds to the Millers Arms in about 1885 reflecting the family's bakery business. The building, purchased by Russells of Gravesend, was pulled down in 1899 and the present pub built. Kidds, who later held it briefly, sold it at a loss to Charringtons in 1924. It is now independent being part of the 1990's enforced sell off of pubs from big brewers' hands.

The King's Head, Bexley, from a watercolour, Scevity was the landlord from 1865-71.

The Millers Arms (on the far side of Bexley High Street) with the George on the right; from a watercolour by I. T. Wilson, c.1865-70.

Railway Tavern/Tower Inn - High Street

*T*he Railway Tavern was formerly the Tower of London though for many years it was simply The Tower Inn. The building is first heard of in the 1681 Manorial Survey and was partly rebuilt at the very beginning of the 18th century. It was first licensed in 1743. In 1756 it was sold to Henry Tasker of Dartford. An addition to the side was rebuilt probably at the time of the arrival of the Dartford Loop line in 1866. After being run for twenty-five years by Michael Staples, son of the founder of the Woodman, Blackfen, the licence was taken over by his son-in-law William Burdett Kelsey. He changed the name to the Tower Inn and Railway Tavern and gradually the Tower Inn part of the name was dropped.

The Railway Tavern, c.1897.

Rising Sun - Vicarage Road

*T*his was founded in 1843 by J B Miskin, the Dartford Brewer. It took the trade of small beerhouses of unknown name further up the road, one of which (possibly supplied by Miskin) was described in the rate book for

The Rising Sun, 1977.

1842 as 'Burnt Out'. The present building dates from 1896. In 1913 it consisted of a centrally located jug and bottle department, a private bar to the right of the door and a public bar on the left with a large bagatelle room behind, and a club room on the first floor. As a child the author can remember visiting the pub after seeing friends in Bexley in the early 1950's and relishing a glass of cold orange sitting at long grey ash tables on the forecourt eating a packet of plain (just potato flavour then) crisps complete with little blue bag of salt.

Bexleyheath, Upton and Barnehurst

Bricklayers Arms - Mayplace Road West

*I*n 1832 Richard Barham junior is recorded as having a beerhouse in Bexley village whilst his father also ran one in Bexleyheath. They were a family of bricklayers. Richard senior's widow Elizabeth was successfully running the pub by 1841. The three cottages on the opposite side of the road built by the Barhams in 1849 are named after her. Her eldest son William, who had been living on the premises, took over the pub's ownership and management in the 1850's. When William temporarily moved to the Builders Arms, Lion Road in 1864/65 his younger brother Richard returned to look after the Bricklayers. In 1871 the brothers lived either side of the Pub in Rose and Box Tree Cottages.

The Bricklayers was rebuilt in 1906.

Coach House/Lord Hill - Watling Street

*T*his was first licensed to James Thompson in September 1815, the year of Waterloo. It commemorates General Rowland Hill who during the Napoleonic wars ranked second only to Wellington in public esteem. Though he has faded from public memory, his was a less anonymous name than the present 'Coach House'. The building has the same dignified

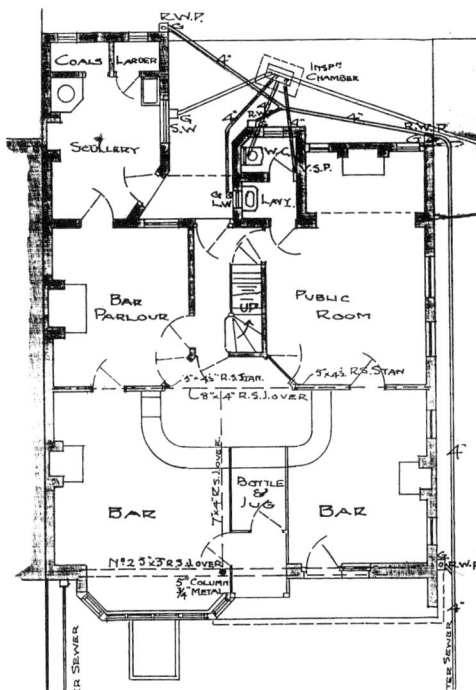

The Bricklayers Arms, part of the plan submitted in 1906 for the rebuilding.

The Lord Hill (now Coach House) c.1900, from a lantern slide.

facade as the original although it now includes the cottage next door.

This pub was sold by the Anglo Bavarian Brewery to Thomas Norfolk of Deptford in 1884 and then via their successors to Trumans.

Trumans also owned the Lord Bexley which stood near Bexleyheath Clock Tower. When the latter closed in 1979 its sign was affixed over the bar of the Lord Hill. The tale is told that when the pub was being revamped in readiness for its change to the Coachhouse, they could not easily remove the Lord Bexley sign and it was consequently boarded over. Hopefully on some future alteration it will be rediscovered (and find its way to our local museum).

Crook Log/Fox & Hounds/Crooked Billet - Crook Log

*T*his may be the site of the oldest pub in the Borough though there are great problems in establishing continuity of licensing. It is sim-

The Crook Log, c.1900.

plest to begin part way through its history as there is known continuous licensing (though numerous name changes) from 1784 when John Elcombe took it over. John Oliver, a Dartford Victualler, took a 21 year lease of the Fox & Hounds at £10 p.a. in 1786 which included a covenant to build within a year stables and also two lodging rooms over the washhouse. The pub and six acres was sold in 1808 to Charles Becket, a Gravesend brewer, for £800. Becket's successors, Russells, exchanged it with Kidds in 1920 who held it briefly before disposing of it to Charringtons.

Though mainly described during the 19th century as the Fox and Hounds it is sometimes referred to as the Crook Log Public House. In the directory for 1882 it is listed as Fox and Hounds but in 1887 under the same landlord it has become 'The Old Crook Log Hotel'. Its dual names continued well into this century.

Its earlier history is more confusing and relates to the heavily wooded surrounding area. This was known as Talehangers, a name meaning a grassy plot for cut firewood at the side of a road. A licensing return for 1605 survives listing four victuallers for Bexley. One of them was Thomas Jackson who in 1608 occupied a substantial property, possibly this site, with 'Otehills, Talehangers and Wevelles' establishing him as the area's first named landlord.

In 1738 the New Cross Turnpike Trust commissioned a survey from Charles Sloane of Gravesend of their road which passed the front of the pub. In it is noted a Crook-log House which could tentatively be calculated as being on the site of the present pub. Frustratingly this 'Crook-log' can be interpreted as licensed premises or just a conspicuous private house. Another name for a short log is a billet and from 1730 to 1753 there was a pub licensed known as the 'Crooked Billet'. It is possible that this is the current building.

Though there may not be continuity from 1605 there are indications of a pub on and around this same site for a considerable time.

Duke of Edinburgh - Broadway

*T*his was built by Kidds of Dartford in 1869 on the site of Reeves Cottage which the brewers had purchased and demolished. Initially it could only trade as an off licence. At the time of writing (1994) it, and its adjacent picturesque cottages, are due for demolition as part of a further Bexleyheath Town Centre redevelopment. Instead of such blanket change it would be nice if these could be kept to reflect changes in style and scale.

The Duke of Edinburgh. 1993. When it became a free house recently the Courage wall sign was removed revealing the original brewers' name.

Earl Haig - Little Heath Road

*F*ield Marshall Earl Haig was from 1915 Allied Commander in Chief in France during the First World War. Though a controversial figure he is now best remembered for the Poppy Fund that bears his name.

Initial plans for an un-named pub to serve the rapidly increasing population of Bexleyheath were passed in 1936. It was not until July 1937 when brewers, Charringtons, had amended plans approved that the pub's name was revealed.

The Earl Haig, 1977.

Golden Lion/Bull - Broadway

A Golden Lion was licensed between 1731-36 and an ale house of that name is noted in the 1738 survey made by the New Cross Turnpike Trust. In a deed of 1761, clearly for the Golden Lion's present site, it is called the Bull. The original building, built some time after 1716 suffered a fire in 1838 and had to be rebuilt. It was sold along with a two acre orchard and stabling for 20 horses in 1875. At a subsequent resale in 1888 it fetched £1,400. The present building dates from 1901.

The landlord in 1869, William Oulton, attracted the attention of a well known local petty thief and fraudster who reacted violently to the landlord's prudent refusal to his request for the loan of a sovereign. When the case came to court the defendant caused considerable amusement by referring to his clean character, his trustworthy nature and his considerable assets (but lack of ready cash to pay his costs).

More recent renovations have sadly seen the removal of a splendid four foot square brilliant-cut and embossed mirror depicting an heraldic lion.

The Golden Lion. The present pub's predecessor in the course of demolition.

Jolly Millers - Mayplace Road West

*T*he Jolly Millers' name originates from the nearby Bexleyheath Windmill which stood two hundred yards away on the north corner of Erith Road and Mayplace Road East. It was built on a greenfield site by the Dartford brewer, William Miskin, in 1862. It expanded into a neighbouring house in 1883 and was sold by Kidds to Charringtons in 1924.

The Jolly Millers shown in a promotional postcard of c.1969.

In 1968 the comedian Jimmy Edwards presented the pub with the Evening Standard 'Town Pub of the Year' award. He arrived in flamboyant style in a horse drawn carriage and blowing a post horn. The pub had been selected from 2,000 nominated by their customers and the judges' difficulty was to decide whether it should be considered in the country or town categories.

Kings Arms - Broadway

*T*his was founded about 1843 by R Markhall as a purpose built pub. He previously ran a beer-house a few doors away and before then a beer-house at Blendon in the early 1830s. The lane adjacent to this corner site pub was marked on the 1862 Ordnance Survey map as Markhalls Lane. The building underwent major alterations in 1935 but for the convenience (or inconvenience) of customers remained open during the works. The author used to visit this pub at lunch times whilst working in Bexleyheath. At that time the Kings Arms still had its art deco embossed windows and an embossed pane advertising Reffells over the entrance to the saloon bar then partly obscured by a modern illuminated box shining out 'Courage'. This fine glass unfortunately was removed during alterations and its where-abouts is unknown. Ind Coope, upon acquisition, closed the pub for seven months in 1984 to carry out a £200,000 refurbishment.

The Kings Arms, c.1951.

Polo Bar/Jolly Drayman/Upton Hotel - Broadway

*T*he Upton Hotel is first recorded in 1869, erected as a purpose built hotel. An immediate application for a spirit licence was made,

The Polo Bar as the Upton Hotel from a (fully used) postcard, c.1900.

the applicants supporting their case by mentioning recent housing development in the area. They received support from the Rev Pincott, the Vicar of Bexleyheath (who was usually in the forefront of opposing licensed premises). He said the establishment met an existing need for sleeping accommodation. The licence was refused this time and again in 1870.

In 1898 plans for major alteration were agreed. The main facade was improved by adding recessed doorways at the opposite ends of the frontage alongside inward curving windows. These doorways served a saloon bar, a small central public bar, and another larger public bar on the right. The space generated by the removal of the staircase along with another room was extended into a 30 ft x 40 ft billiard room. This must have been a great success because within six months further plans were passed which increased the depth of the billiard room to some 52 ft.

The pub was refitted in a psychedelic style for the young in 1970 but this was not a success. It reopened after another refit as the Jolly Drayman in July 1973. It was renamed the Polo Bar in the early 1990's.

Prince Albert - Broadway

*T*he pub is named in honour of Prince Albert, the husband of Queen Victoria, who had been a leading promoter of the Great Exhibition of 1851.

The Prince Albert from a lantern slide, c.1900.

This large purpose-built, fully licensed establishment was constructed in 1851 by Joseph Amos. Born in 1812, by the 1850's he was a successful builder employing twelve men. He owned brickfields and had his home and counting house in nearby Sherston Place. Amos sold it to Thomas Norfolk of Deptford in 1877.

Landlord Thomas Harding was the first local publican to be summoned in 1903 under the new Child Messenger Act. He was charged with selling short measured, improperly sealed intoxicating liquor to a minor, one Annie Ellis, a girl under the age of 14. Her mother was also summoned for sending her. Annie had been stopped by the police coming out of the pub at 10.40 a.m. (!) on 25th January. Questioned about the part filled pint bottle she was carrying (the Act had specified a minimum quantity of one pint) she told the officer she had been sent with three halfpence to fetch stout and also admitted her age. In consideration of the newness of the Act the magistrates only fined the landlord a sum equal to the costs (with a kindly note that it wouldn't be remembered against him at next licensing session) and the mother's case was dismissed and costs remitted. Both were warned about future conduct.

Red Barn - Barnehurst Road

Permission to build this pub was granted in the summer of 1936. The pub is celebrated as the home of the revival of traditional jazz in Britain. In 1944 George Webb, a worker at Vickers, Crayford, and his friends would play jazz for relaxation. They formed a group

The Red Barn, c.1988.

known as 'George Webb's Dixielanders' and performed jamming sessions on Monday nights at the Red Barn. They soon had an increasing following in the music which had its roots in New Orleans half a century earlier. On 4th July 1985 the well known jazz player, George Melly, unveiled a plaque to commemorate the pub's and their involvement in this revival.

Robin Hood & Little John - Lion Road,

*A*t the end of 1851 lands near Bexleyheath owned by the Lewin family of The Hollies, Sidcup were being sold. A 'New Bexley Freehold Land Society' was formed to promote building in the area although it enjoyed only limited success. John Moors, a shoemaker from East Wickham, purchased three plots and in 1854 built the Robin Hood fronting Lion Road. Within three years he had split off half the land to build four cottages on Lewin Road. Trade could not have been that good because he carried on his shoemaking business from the pub. It is called the Robin Hood in the 1861 census and the rate books add Little John in 1865.

The Robin Hood and Little John; note the bottle and jug department accessed through the ornate classically styled doorcase, c.1925.

Rose - Broadway

*T*he present building of 1955 replaced the original of 1834 which was destroyed by a bomb in 1941. William Butler, the builder, worked as landlord until his death in 1859. Although the pub was only small he was employing an ostler/potboy in 1851. Ownership passed to his widow and then sons,

The Rose from a lantern slide, c.1935.

Richard and John, the founders of the adjacent 'Bexley Heath Circular and Frame Sawing Mills'.

Beasleys took a lease on it in the 1880's.

Royal Oak (Polly Clean Stairs)/ Woodman - Mount Road

*T*his charming brick and weather boarded building has one of the most colourful nicknames of any pub in the borough. The 'Polly Clean Stairs', by which devoted regulars may exclusively know it, is derived from a house-proud lady who washed the front steps every day. She has been conclusively identified as Mary Ann Elms, the second wife of the landlord Robert Elms whom she married in 1838. She continued to run the pub after his death in 1865 until 1894. Their son Henry went on to manage the Three Blackbirds in Blendon which sixty years previously had been run by his father's (first) in-laws.

Local landowners, the Russell family, erected three adjacent farm cottages in 1827 and George Crafter occupied the one that fronted Alers Road. By 1837, in addition to his main occupation of chandler, he became a beer retailer, calling his establishment 'The Woodman'. Robert Elms took the property over in 1842 and by 1851 he had renamed it the Royal Oak. He later moved the pub to the cottage fronting Mount Road.

The Farnborough brewers, Fox and Son, bought the property in 1854 and for some years it is described incorrectly in rate books as the Fox Inn. Fox and Son came into financial difficulties around the turn of the century and

21

the Royal Oak was auctioned in 1909 for £1,620. It was one of the few premises they were successful in selling. Fox was succeeded as proprietor by Charles Beasley of the North Kent Brewery in Plumstead.

The Royal Oak, c.1910.

Royal Standard - Lion Road

*A*lfred Ayers founded this pub in 1864 though the rate books call it The Standard Inn. The building is well positioned, impressively closing the view along Standard Road; second only in desirability to a corner site. Its visual impact was improved during alterations in 1910 when an ornate new front was added.

The Royal Standard dominating the view along Standard Road, c.1988.

Travellers Home - Long Lane

*T*he origin of the name derives from the fact that travellers and hawkers would park up their caravans on land in this area.

During 1851 Robert Mann, himself a licensed hawker, erected four cottages on a triangle of land he had purchased in 1847. The two right hand cottages were combined to create the pub. The first recorded licensee is Thomas Leggatt in 1854. A further two cottages were erected in 1860.

Henry Pease, a local market gardener who had purchased all the land and premises from Robert Mann, was unable to meet his mortgage terms and his lender, a Dartford solicitor, repossessed and sold the property in 1868 to

The Travellers Home, 1934.

Alexander Walker, a Gravesend brewer, for £445. Walker set about building a much larger pub further to the north west and granted a fresh twenty-one year lease to the existing licensee, James Goldsmith. This arrangement was not entirely successful as shortly afterwards Goldsmith was persuaded to surrender the lease. In 1903 Charringtons acquired the brewery from Walker's trustees.

Though this (second) pub was demolished in 1935 to make way for the current building, numbers 48 and 50 Long Lane, an earlier Travellers Home still survive.

Volunteer - Church Road

*T*his was originally a private home and it only became a pub in 1868 when a Mr Norton became the landlord. Serious objections were raised in 1873 to a renewal of the licence on the death of the landlord, Mr Smale. Residents of Church Road complained at the level of drunkenness and the disturbances created by a low class of clientele. The objectors' solicitor commented on the regular trouble the police were caused and that Mr Smale had been fined 10 shillings (50p) for selling drink during illegal hours. Nevertheless the licence was renewed.

In 1936 the then brewery landlords, Reffells, built a matching gabled extension increasing the pub area by half.

The Volunteer, c.1988.

William Camden - Avenue Road

*T*his was named after the eminent antiquarian, William Camden, who published a survey of the nation's antiquities at the early date of 1586. In 1621 he purchased the Manor of Bexley so that he could grant its considerable rental income to the University of Oxford to endow a professorship of history.

Like other pubs planned after the war, there was a considerable delay before ideas were realised. Though original plans by Whitbreads' architects had been approved in 1949 there were various amendments and it was not until late 1956 that the premises were completed.

The half built William Camden, 1956.

Woodman - Watling Street

Policeman Joseph Moreton occupied these old premises which were used for his wife's millinery business. However, by 1863 he had left the police force, converted the shop to a beerhouse and became the first landlord of the Woodman.

In 1985 the publican was way ahead of his time. He announced that he had 'plans to instal a Japanese singing machine which plays background music of many hit records - and by using the song sheets customers can provide the vocals'. Should he be congratulated or condemned?

The Woodman, shortly before World War II.

Wrong 'Un - Broadway

The latest pub in Bexley London Borough opened in June 1994 in a property last used as a furniture shop. The name is an unfortunate use of a 'foreign' term to do with cricket. In

The Wrong 'Un, 1994.

this locale of course a 'Wrong-'Un' is a criminal: a case of a people divided by a common language. I hope the name doesn't attract the wrong clientele. Wetherspoons, the progressive pub chain owners, run some very attractive pubs many of them incorporating 'Moon' in their name. It is a pity that they did not think of a former Bexleyheath establishment and call it 'The Red Moon Re-Risen'. Research showed that the land on which it is built was at one time a cricket ground, hence the pub's internal decor, so I suppose they could have called it the 'Owzat' with a sign of a cricket ball being hit over the moon.

Yacht - Long Lane

*P*lans for a new pub in Bexleyheath had been approved in 1937. They were submitted by the Dartford Brewery which had been working since 1924 under the joint auspices of Style and Winch of Maidstone and the Royal Brewery, Brentford whom from 1929 had been working in association with Barclay Perkins of Southwark. Once built, it obtained a licence removed from the Yacht on the waterfront in Erith High Street which was due to be demolished as part of a road widening scheme in the town centre, thus explaining the name of this beached vessel far from water.

The Yacht, just prior to opening, 1938.

Blackfen, Blendon and Bridgen

Blue Anchor (Snake and Pickaxe)/ Anchor and Cable - Bridgen Road

*T*his was a charming but tiny pub the subject of numerous photographers. Its location in the hamlet of Bridgen epitomised Bexley's rural past that survived into the inter-war years.

Its history is a long one. In 1681 it was known as the Anchor and Cable, from 1713 to 1726 as just the Anchor and from 1729 onwards as the Blue Anchor though it had the more sinister nickname of the Snake and Pickaxe derived from the sign's design.

The Blue Anchor, c.1910.

Up to the 1920's it catered for the 80 or so inhabitants of the hamlet along with trade from travellers and the surrounding district. Against a background of an anticipated growth in population and the building's terminally poor physical condition, Major Phillips of the Dartford Brewery Company told the licensing magistrates in 1927 that the pub would have to be demolished. The brewery had already acquired a suitable vacant plot opposite for the planned replacement. Concern was expressed that the proposed new larger pub could also advertise itself on the newly built Rochester Way and would be 'visited by charabanc parties from the East End of London and so on and causing noises on Sundays'! With suitable assurances from the brewery and despite the magistrates fondness for the old establishment they agreed to the change. The new pub, erected in 1928, increased trade considerably and therefore the saloon was substantially enlarged in 1935.

The old building became the Bridgen Cafe but it and the adjacent cottages were demolished within a few years.

Jolly Fenman - Blackfen Road

*T*he site for the intended pub was acquired in the late 1930's and plans were soon approved. However during wartime the funds of brewers, Watneys, seem to have been diverted to

Jolly Fenman, 1977.

pay for repairs to existing damaged pubs. Various plans of 1940, 1948, 1950 and 1954 came and went. The pub was finally completed in early 1957.

In August 1984 the pub was extended to create a brewery. A glass screen allowed a view from the saloon into the area where Blackfen Bitter and Fenman Fortune Ale were being brewed. However, fortunes were not made and brewing ceased after just a few years.

Three Blackbirds - Blendon

*T*his pub was licensed as far back as 1717. For a good number of years the freehold rested with the successive owners of Blendon Hall, an old country house demolished in 1934. It was sold in 1921 for £4,400 and then passed to Charringtons twenty years later.

The roof and interior however, are more modern as the pub unfortunately suffered a serious fire at the turn of the century which gutted it.

The single storey extension to the front left is late Victorian and was used as a club room. The pub was extended by a third in 1983 to provide extra catering capacity.

The Three Blackbirds, the immediate aftermath of the fire that all but destroyed it, c.1900.

The Woodman - Blackfen Road

The founder of this pub, George Staples, first appears locally as landlord of the Blue Anchor, Bridgen from 1838 to 1841. He then moved to a small house near Apple Pie Corner, the local name for the junction of Parkhill and Upton Roads, opposite the 100 acres of Bexley Woods which he rented from the University of Oxford until 1857. He must have been successful at this for in 1845 he could afford to have the Woodman, Blackfen built, celebrating his occupation in the pub's name. These dual occupations were continued by his son William who had succeeded him by 1863 as landlord and who ran the pub with his bride, 19 years his junior.

Local brewers Reffells leased the pub from 1899 and it was not until the summer of 1930 that they acquired the freehold. Even before negotiations were complete plans for a projected rebuild were being drawn up. The present pub was erected behind the old in 1931 and only then was the original demolished allowing continuity of business. It is an excellent design by Kenneth Dalgliesh who also designed property locally at Old Forge Way, Sidcup and elsewhere. His initials are set in a small stone block alongside the entrance to the public bar. On the Westwood Lane facade are the initials of Percy Hugh Waistell, the then Managing Director of Reffells Brewery, Bexley and John Alfred Harvey, the established landlord also known locally for keeping a pet goose.

In 1938 the dining hall was enlarged and the saloon bar extended. The original window frames were reused to retain the same atmosphere as the original design.

Until recently the Woodman possessed two inn signs. That next to the traffic lights was a rare example of fretted tin depicting a woodman wielding a axe at a tree. Its present whereabouts is unknown.

The author's late mother was a barmaid here working for Mr & Mrs Abbott. Whenever the author's father called here for a pint she was meticulous in NOT serving him. She always did it to prevent any possible speculation about measure etc. The author has fond memories of occasionally sitting outside with a soft drink and a '1d.' arrowroot biscuit. They seemed about four inches in diameter but gradually were made smaller and the author changed custom to Meredith & Drew wafers. On rare occasions fish and chips were bought on the way home.

The Woodman, (or Woodmen), Blackfen showing the almost complete new building and the old one around which Kenneth Dalgliesh designed the replacement, 1931.

Crayford, Northend and Slade Green

Bear and Ragged Staff/Half Moon - London Road

Crayford had a Bear and Ragged Staff listed in its licensing records from 1704 to 1720 but its site is unknown. A pub on the present corner site goes back a considerable time although it was at one time known as the Half Moon. This name was mentioned in a deed of 1684 when it was transferred from Mr Sprig to J Marsham and in 1698 from Sir Robert Marsham to Sir Cloudsley Shovell. Sir John Walden was licensee from 1713 and when he died in February 1728 his widow Mary appears to have renamed it The Bear and Ragged Staff. The following licensee, Luke Percival, paid rent of £13 p.a. to the Manor of Howbury. By 1744 it was the most successful pub in Crayford, a position it retained until the establishment of the Bell.

In April 1786 John Hards, a successful corn miller of Dartford, caused excitement when he came into the pub and claimed that he had shot someone who had tried to rob him. The incident was alleged to have happened whilst he was travelling down Bexley-Heath Hill. John Hards was known to be a courageous man and his business often meant he had to travel home late from town through roads where highwaymen hid. Three footpads attacked him and as one tried to grab his horse's bridle, John Hards leant forward and shot him. He rapidly escaped, miraculously avoiding the shots of the other two assailants. This was confirmed the following day when a man was found nearby,

barely alive, with a bad throat wound which had been bleeding all night. His companions, thinking him dead, had robbed him of his money and silver shoe buckles. His wound was stitched up and in the final days that he lingered he confessed to other crimes. He was a local man and the burial register for St Paulinus notes '6th April 1786, James Smith, shot in attempting to rob Mr Hards on Bexley Heath'.

James Saxton was licensee from 1810. He expanded the business and also traded as a wine merchant further up London Road. The wine store continued as an independent concern from 1853 until the 1890's, becoming Lyles Mineral Water Works in 1902.

The Bear and Ragged Staff, called the Old Bear and Staff in 1907.

The Court Baron or annual meeting of the Manor of Newbery was held at the pub in 1851 when £4.10s.0d. of the £21 collected was spent on a dinner.

It became a Beasleys' pub in 1886 and was pulled down and rebuilt by them in 1925. Its name, which had undergone a number of confusing minor variations, was then standardised to the Bear and Ragged Staff.

Boundary/Plough/PunchBowl/ Threadbare Castle - Northend Road

A pub has stood on this site for a considerable time. In a change of ownership of the pub in 1834 an early deed was 'recited' but frustratingly no date was mentioned though it would relate prior to 1710 when we first have a confirmed licence of the Plough. It transferred

The Boundary, 1988.

'All that messuage tenement or dwelling house formerly called or known by the name of Threadbare Castle otherwise Symonds Field House but now and for many years past called or known by the sign of the Plough together with the shed and stable thereunto belonging'.

For most of its life (and even still to locals) it was known as the Plough. When a Benjamin Harvey, who had run the pub in the 1730's, moved to alternative premises in Crayford he took the name with him. He hoped no doubt that trade and reputation of the Northend Plough would follow him, that any traveller asking for the Plough would be directed to his new premises. It was at this time that Thomas Berry, who had succeeded him at Northend, used the sign of The Punch Bowl. However when Benjamin Harvey moved in 1747, Thomas Berry changed back to the name Plough making two of that name in the parish.

Over the years the pub had absorbed some cottages into its structure but this was insufficient to meet modern requirements. In 1936, Kidds, the brewers, owned the pub and adjacent shop and two cottages. After paying the shop proprietor compensation of £25 (plus £10 removal expenses) they set about rebuilding and opened in time for the Christmas trade 1937. The modern premises were renamed the Boundary in 1986. The boundary referred to is that of a few yards away dividing the old parishes of Erith to the north and the 'Northend' of Crayford Parish to the south.

Corner Pin - Slade Green Road

*T*his was built by the Stoneham family, the local landowners in 1844, at one end of a terrace of six farm labourers' cottages called Poplar Place. It was probably named after a

The Corner Pin showing the new extension to the front, c.1907.

pin in the then popular game of nine pin skittles. It was run in the early 1860's by Charles Hearn, the father of James Hearn who was then running the Lord Raglan. James, after a spell in an Erith beerhouse came back in 1882 to Slade Green, and this time to the Corner Pin.

The old pub expanded into one of the cottages next door and by the end of the century had a single storey extension put across the front. Although Watneys had permission to rebuild the pub in 1947 they did not do so until 1958.

Crayford Arms - High Street

*T*he corner of High Street and Bexley Lane was redeveloped in November 1864 with the building of one large house and three small cottages. By the early part of 1865 two more cottages had been built and the large house was divided into two. One part was let as the beer-shop and the other part, a house, shop and garden was let later in the year. By 1869 these two parts seem to have merged back together. The pub was acquired from the first owners in the 1870's by Crowley, a Croydon brewery. In 1936, the then owners, Reffells, extended the building further in to Bexley Lane.

The arms depicted on the present sign are those of the Draper family who owned the Manors of Howbury & Newbery of Crayford and the Drapers Place Estate of Erith and Bexleyheath until the early 17th century. There is a fine tomb in St Paulinus Church to the Drapers.

The Crayford Arms; a lively view of the High Street. The pub, on the right, is on the corner of a very narrow Bexley Lane, 1889.

Duke of Wellington - London Road

*T*his was the first of four beerhouses in what is now a conservation area and, with the recent conversion of the Lord Nelson to a restaurant, the sole survivor.

In 1850 Robert Fordham had started a beerhouse amongst the factories in Barnes Cray. No doubt sensing more opportunity on a main road he moved here in April 1853 to become first landlord of this newly erected pub. After five years he moved on to the established Corner Pin for a couple of years. By 1870 he was at (and possibly the first landlord of) the New Marsh Tavern on Erith marshes. He was no doubt related to James Fordham who had a beerhouse in the High Street and to Thomas and Sarah who ran the Harrow at North End.

This pub possesses some nice old pub enamel signs advertising Reids beer.

The Duke of Wellington, 1975, showing the central entrance, later bricked up.

Dukes Head - High Street

*T*he present building dates from 1926 replacing a pub first licensed to Peter Pyne in 1771. For many years from the 1820's it was owned by the Dwelly family who carried on a black-

The Dukes Head, Crayford High Street again, this time looking uphill, 1905.

smith's trade in the yard. It was leased in 1859 by the Deptford brewers, Thomas Norfolk & Sons.

Excitement was caused in 1899 when 'Potty', the pub's man of all trades, was digging vegetables in the back garden and unearthed a coffin! The landlord was called, then the police who decided to open it on the spot. It was found to contain the mortal remains of the previous landlord's favourite cat.

Harrow - Northend Road

*T*his lay back from the road surrounded by an orchard and was established by John Killick before 1838. It was owned by Frederick Barne and leased in 1893 to Russells Gravesend Brewery.

It was rebuilt in 1904 and enlarged in 1936 in a carefully matching style.

The Harrow in 1938 showing the 1936 additions; an enlarged saloon to the right and games room to the left.

Jolly Farmers - Thames Road

James Upton was the first landlord of this pub which was built by Miles Barne, the landowner, in 1830 to take swift advantage of the Beerhouse Act of that year. The area in which it is located was for many years known as the Saw Mills. Before the last war the pub was in Iron Mill Lane. It stood in the short section of Iron Mill Lane that was absorbed into the newly built Thames Road, hence the change in its address (but not location). Directories from 1851, the probable year of rebuilding, describe James Upton as a 'Farmer' so perhaps his profits had made him 'jolly' enough to expand his activities. His son George took over by 1870 and was still there in early 1891. It was later owned by Russells of Gravesend.

The Jolly Farmers, also showing the mill pond and buildings in the background, c.1900.

Lord Raglan - Hazel Road

*F*ield Marshal Lord Raglan lost an arm at Waterloo and his life in 1855 at Sebastopol in the Crimea War. He gave his name to this pub which was built in the year of his death. It was built and owned by William Killick and initially leased to Jesse Hearn until Norfolk and Sons of Deptford acquired it in 1858. The old Raglan was pulled down together with the three cottages to the north and a new pub erected on the site in 1900.

The Lord Raglan, c. 1898, as interesting as the old pub building are the bicycle, shotgun and the publicans, proud owners of the pony and trap.

One Bell - Old Road

*T*here was a pub of this name in Crayford in 1700 but this earlier establishment has no connection with the present one.

The present Bell or One Bell as it later became known was a purpose built pub

The One Bell, 1988.

erected in 1770. The licensee for the first three years was Richard Sevenoaks but he appears to have then put in licensed managers until 1794 when he returned. The owner in 1780 is recorded in the Land Tax as Mr Hussey. The Husseys have some relationship to the Hussey Fleets Brewers of Dartford. The latter were involved in brewing from the mid-1770's when they took over the Pettets' brewery.

The Universal British Directory of 1792 notes that in Crayford 'the principal inn is the Bell where the Gravesend stage stops to change horses'. At this time London Road was not yet built and the main Dover Road from London ran over Bexleyheath, down Watling Street, along Old Road past the Bell, down the High Street and on through Dartford.

Railway Tavern - Forest Road

*T*his was built as part of a major development by the South Eastern Railway Company in Slade Green. Planned, though only incompletely realised, were sheds capable of holding 300 engines and accommodation for 370 families. The hotel was designed to cater for both commercial travellers and railway officials. The licensing authorities had reservations about its design judging there to be too many public entrances (and exits) and poorly laid out bar areas. They only approved a provisional licence in 1898 when modifications were made and the railway company gave the assurance that they would retain control of the building.

Although the licence when granted was on the understanding that the pub would be strictly under the management of the South Eastern Railway, the Dartford Brewery Company purchased it in February 1922.

The Railway Tavern, 1988.

Royal Charlotte/Royal George - Station Road

*T*he Royal George was erected in 1854 by J Durrant and stood by the present railway bridge. In 1864 his widow disposed of the pub either to the Dartford brewer Miskin or direct to The South Eastern Railway Company. The S.E.R. were preparing to construct the Dartford Loop Line and may have intended to demolish the pub upon acquisition. A new building was built for Miskins in Dartford Heath Lane, as Station Road was then known.

Harriet Masters, the licensee of the closed building, continued in charge of the new. The original building in fact survived to become the home of a railway employee. The cellar doors could still be seen until it was finally demolished recently.

Although the first landlord of the Royal George was a Charlotte, the new pub was given the name of the Royal Charlotte in celebration not of her but of Queen Charlotte, the wife of George III.

The Royal Charlotte, c.1910.

White Swan / & Railway Tavern - Crayford Road

*T*he origins of a pub on this site go back to at least 1726 and maybe to the 17th century. It has been called the Swan or White Swan at various times but one licensing record for 1716 confusingly notes both names.

In 1874 Richard Blackman of the 'Swan Inn & Railway Tavern' was summonsed for holding a fair on the 22nd August in a field he occupied without lawful authority. He insisted it was a fair 'established by custom' and was keen that it should continue since the stall rents that he collected were equivalent to the rent he paid on his pub. His solicitor successfully defended the action by producing a certified copy of the original Charter establishing Crayford Fair.

In 1908 the pub came near to being closed permanently. It was announced at the annual February licensing sessions that the lease on the pub was due to expire at Michaelmas and the freeholder, a gentleman of strong views on the question of Temperance, did not wish to renew the lease. Until now he had accepted the rents but this provided the opportunity of ceasing to be the recipient of any monies from the licensed trade. The Dartford Brewery Company who leased the pub tried to purchase the freehold without success. The bench thought that this was a chance of extinguishing a licence without opposition. The brewery had also acquired cottages opposite and asked for the removal of the licence to premises about to be constructed on that site which the bench agreed to. The plan, in fact, came to nothing as the pub managed to continue on its original site.

The pub was acquired by the independent chain, J T Davies and Son, in 1967 and fourteen years later they built a new pub behind the old.

The White Swan, c.1900.

Erith

Cross Keys - High Street

A John Draper is recorded as licensee of a Cross Keys from 1749 - 1751 but it is unclear if these are earlier, unconnected premises.

This pub is one of only four surviving in Bexley known to have issued tokens. Uses of tokens were many and varied. They were a form of currency, sometimes denominated. They were sometimes given in lieu of a drink to persons who didn't want to share in a round that moment, but would have the drink that was purchased for them later. They were also used in skittle alleys to give to the person resetting the pins; or were sometimes purchased at a discount to give to members of a society meeting at the pub that night. They were essentially a means of securing continued custom to a pub.

They were issued at the Cross Keys by the landlord, Nelson Ambrose, who ran the pub for twenty years from the late 1860's. In his time the pub consisted of a bar, bar parlour, tap room, bagatelle room, smoking room, kitchen, underground cellar, three bedrooms and two attics with detached pot house with a loft above, coal shed and poultry house and also a boat builders yard with a covered workshop, the roof of which formed a large platform overlooking the river.

This Cross Keys suffered a severe fire on Monday 10th August 1891. Two young coalies working at Beadle Bros' wharf near the Cross Keys platform saw a fire in the bagatelle room at about 4 a.m. Unable to awaken the landlady or staff by banging on the doors one of them managed to climb from the outside up into the first floor bedroom of the landlady, Mrs Kate Harvey. They alerted the other occupants but 'the building being old and the stairs of a peculiar nature' they were unable to escape and had to descend to the street by ladder. The Erith Fire Brigade arrived within fifteen minutes and the Bexleyheath Brigade an hour later. The fire, which destroyed the building, nearly spread to cottages in Cross Keys Yard but the inhabitants managed to get their furniture into the street. Many of the surrounding premises were old, highly combustible buildings.

Although Mrs Harvey had been negotiating the sale of the property - she was even expecting a deposit to be placed that Monday - it was she who reopened the new Cross Keys. Rebuilding commenced in the following February and it re-opened on 1st August, Bank Holiday Monday 1892. She had remarried and the adverts note that there was special catering for yachting parties, unrivalled views of the river from balconies and terraces, and dancing on the platform.

The Cross Keys showing the pub as rebuilt in 1892. This view of the High Street, also showing the White Hart, was taken before the High Pavement was demolished in 1900.

Nordenfeldt (Pom-Pom) - Erith Road

*E*ven before this pub existed Watney Coombe & Reid knew they wanted to name it the Nordenfeldt Tavern as it was designed to serve employees of the adjacent and large Maxim Nordenfeldt Gun and Ammunition Company. Its nickname the 'Pom Pom' is a reference to the 1899 Maxim automatic quick firing gun.

Their first licence application in 1898 was refused. They applied again in 1899 and substantiated their claim by drawing attention to the rapid increase in Erith's population (from 9,000 in 1881, to 13,000 in 1891, and 17,000 in 1898 to 19,000 in 1899) and the building of 260 houses within a half mile radius of the site. One resident, a customs officer, remarked on the new houses' distance from licensed premises, and said to the amusement of the assembly that he had sent a girl to the Ship Inn for beer to accompany his meal but by the time she returned over an hour later his family had finished dinner.

The railway provided a formidable access problem for residents of the new streets as to reach the town (and a pub) it could only be crossed at the level crossing at Pembroke Road or by using the private tunnel that carried the light rail to Parish's Quarry.

The Nordenfeldt, c.1910.

The bench, whilst recognising the needs of the neighbourhood, thought that overall there were still too many licences in Erith. There were six within one hundred yards in the High Street and they would prefer one of those to be surrendered before granting a licence to the Nordenfeldt. In the following year, despite an ever larger 'dry' population and the offer of two licences, the bench still refused the application.

In 1901 a shop was built facing onto Riverdale Road which is now part of the present pub. In August that year Thomas Knight, the occupier of the shop, made three connected applications. The first was for a full licence and, failing that, just a beer licence for the proposed pub and, if these two failed, then for an off-licence for the shop where he resided. They were opposed, as usual, by the licensed trade and additionally by the Temperance movement in the form of the newly erected non-conformist churches. The Erith and Belvedere Free Church Council and in particular the Trustees of the Primitive Methodist Chapel, which had been erected opposite in Riverdale Road the year before, objected. Their objection was over-ruled on the grounds that they knew perfectly well that the plot had been reserved for a public house when they set about their own building. Rather, the bench still required the surrender of a licence in an

area of the town where they were too dense. The brewers, impatient, and with money tied up in the land for three years (and the magistrates seemingly intractable) surrendered a licence acceptable to the magistrates and the Nordenfeldt was granted a provisional licence.

Royal Alfred - Manor Road

*T*he Shipwrecked Mariners Society provided funds for the purchase of the local mansion Belvedere House in 1865 to be run by an independent committee as 'The Belvedere Institution for Worn Out & Disabled Merchant Seamen'. The pub name celebrates the fact that Prince Alfred became its patron in 1866 whereupon the title was changed to the Royal Alfred Merchant Seamans Institution.

In several instances the pub is referred to as the 'Prince' Alfred, even in some official records, but this is just a confusion with the pub of that name in Belvedere.

The Royal Alfred, 1988.

It was built in 1866 on land known as 'The Racefield' and was leased to a local business-man, Mr G F Webber.

William Stephens obtained an underlease in 1875 for the then substantial sum of £2,800. He raised £1,600 by loan from Truman & Co and of course would have been tied to sell their beer. He was succeeded in 1878 by James Cooke, one of the few local publicans known to have issued tokens. The brass tokens were in the values of 1d., 2d., 3d. and 6d. and were issued prior to his assigning his lease to Beasleys of Plumstead in 1891.

In 1916 when plans for additions were being made we have sight of the layout of the bars and unusually some bar fittings. The entrance in Appold Street led into a small private bar to the right, whilst to the left was the saloon with another bar parlour. The corner entrance led into a small bar looking out over Manor Road. The Manor Road entrance led straight into the public bar and from there to a tap room. The square counter that the bars surrounded had a six-pull beer engine and in the middle an island stillion. The corner bars do not show a method of heating, whereas the saloon bar and tap room were both heated by fireplaces and the public bar had a central stove.

Running Horses - High Street

This can be dated to at least 1810 when a John Kempton or Kimpton held a licence. In the 1840's the pub looked across the High Street to where the river lapped the edges of the road. Within twenty years the river was made more distant by infilling of wharves. Later, buildings were erected blocking the view - the more so

in 1903 when Cannon & Gaze rebuilt their flour mills following a fire.

In 1874 the Lesney Park Sale Catalogue notes that the pub was substantially built and contained five bars and parlours, had a large clubroom on the first floor with two bedrooms and a further five bedrooms on the second. It failed, however, to reach its reserve price and was privately sold in 1877. Four weeks later an eighty year lease was granted to Harriet Bridge, the widow of James Bridge, who had moved from the White Hart to this pub in 1870. The cost was £700 of which £500 had already been spent and £200 was covenanted to be spent on new buildings. She recouped her considerable investment when she retired and

The Running Horses also showing the effects of World War II bomb damage as it appeared in the late 1940's.

granted an underlease to Crowleys of Croydon in 1879.

Erith Council undertook major redevelopment of the riverside in 1938, involving widening the High Street and therefore demolishing old premises including pubs. The old pub now lies partly under the road, pavement and car park to the north west of the present one. The work, however, reopened the river vista.

The pub was damaged in 1940 by a bomb and although the licensee was unfortunately killed his widow continued operating from temporary buildings set up in the rear of the pub. The damage was repaired by 1946 which was very quick considering shortages of materials and in comparison with the Rose at Bexleyheath and the Horse and Groom, Sidcup.

It was extensively altered in 1974, which reduced the number of downstairs bars but created a large restaurant upstairs.

Ship - West Street

*T*his probably started in 1859 with the arrival of John Warner, a one time calico printer, who had been running a beerhouse at

Northend. He left the Ship in 1861 going on to manage various other pubs locally.

Day Noakes & Co., the brewers, had an interest in the pub from 1895 and shortly after acquiring the freehold in 1927 had plans approved for renovating the interior. These reveal that the Ship may be one of those unusual properties that have what is known as Flying Freehold. This is where one of their bedrooms leading from the top of the main stairs sat on top of the next door shop below.

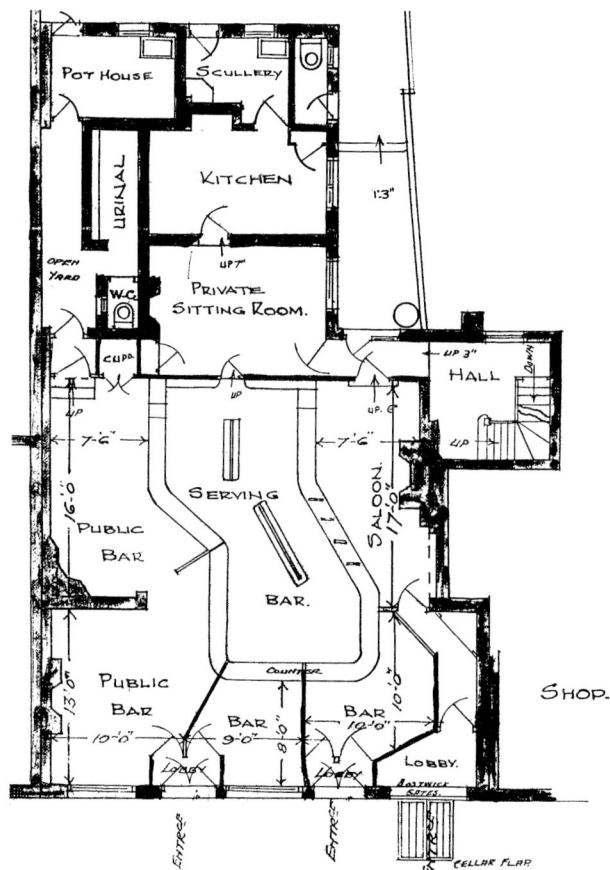

The Ship, a ground plan of the bar areas, 1927, with a 'wobbly U'-shaped counter (to make drunken seamen feel at home?)

Trafalgar - West Street

*T*his appears to be established in 1862 with William Ashby recorded as a beer retailer of an unnamed house in West Street. In the same directory a John Ashby is recorded at the Ship. They were probably related and there is the possibility that they were co-partners in the Ship. It was taken over by 1865 by James Upton, one of the sons of the long-time land-lord of the Old Jolly Farmers, Saw Mills, Crayford. His daughter, Anna Morgan, embellished its then plain facade in 1899 by the addition of regency style bay windows rather reminiscent of seaside towns.

The Trafalgar, the front elevation before the addition of the Regency style windows, 1899.

White Hart - High Street

*T*his is considerably older than many of Erith's pubs as the earliest recorded licence for the White Hart is in 1715 granted to a Stephen Dilley. It is possible that the White Hart may date back to 1707 when Dilley was appointed by Erith Manor Court, a now redundant body that oversaw much of the town's affairs, as one of two ale conners or quality testers.

Apart from two tap rooms, bar and bar parlour the building in 1874 also contained a covered skittle alley and a brick built store used as a soda water and ginger beer manufactuary.

J Bridge who was here in the 1860's issued an undenominated token for this pub. James had founded the Halfway House in 1866 and then gone to the Chequers, Picardy Hill between 1867-1870 and subsequently to the Running Horses, Erith.

Mr Harry Lippard, a licensee, suffered a bicycle accident that prevented him attending the annual licensing session in 1901. He suffered head injuries and was confined to a lunatic asylum. The magistrates were in a quandary on how to deal with the situation. They had clear guidelines in cases of death with automatic protection of licence to the spouse of the deceased. Indeed if the property was transferred mid year the then transferee had protection until the next licensing or mid term transfer session when they could judge whether his character met licensing criteria. In this peculiar circumstance they were confronted with a licensee who was very much alive but unable to indicate that he wished to renew. After two adjourned meetings to see if there was any improvement in his condition they noted that they would close the pub on 15th October and appoint a committee to make an assignment of the licence. His brother Thomas took over and ran it for four years. The old pub and a cottage next door were demolished and the present building erected in 1902.

The White Hart, 1901.

Belvedere, Abbey Wood and Thamesmead

Barge Pole - Coralline Walk

*T*his community orientated pub was built in the early 1970's as part of Area 1 of Thamesmead.

The Barge Pole, 1994.

Belvedere Hotel - Picardy Road

*T*his was built in about 1860 'regardless of expense' as superior premises to serve as a Railway Hotel. Its name came to be more widely known as a result of the tragic and dramatic event of lst October 1864 when a gunpowder barge exploded on the Thames as it was making a delivery to one of the powder magazines on Erith Marshes. The percussion caused further detonations blowing up nearly fifty tons of explosives. It caused widespread

destruction to the surrounding area breaking plate glass in pubs as far away as Dartford; even the window frames themselves in the Belvedere Hotel were destroyed. Whilst soldiers hastily summoned from the Woolwich garrison worked speedily to repair the destroyed section of river wall before the next high tide the remains of the victims were conveyed to the Hotel. Special trains were laid on from London Bridge for the thousands of sightseers who came to Belvedere. A newspaper

CARRYING THE SUFFERERS TO THE BELVIDERE HOTEL.

The Belvedere Hotel being used as a makeshift mortuary for the victims of the Erith gunpowder explosion in 1864.

said 'Excepting the kitchen and tap room all the apartments were rendered untenable but nevertheless it may be safely affirmed that the house never did such a business before as it has done since the calamity which so shattered it.' At the Coroner's inquest in the large Clubroom upstairs they had to board up the window openings to keep out the wind.

A later landlord, Samuel Gibson was summoned in 1874 for selling beer in a place other than which he was licensed. One day, at half past eleven, a retired police constable was just outside The Diamond Fuel factory about a mile from the Hotel. There a man was selling beer to workmen and he joined them and purchased some for himself. For the purpose of entrapment he called again in the afternoon and after three o'clock the beer cart, containing eighteen gallons and some bottles, arrived. He, again with other men from the factory, purchased some beer. He reported the matter to the Excise authorities who warned Mr Gibson that it was illegal according to his licence to sell off his premises unless the drinks had been ordered previously. In court Mr Gibson was able to prove that he had a standing order from the factory proprietors for beer and tobacco. The arrangement was made so that the workmen didn't waste time away from the factory going for beer. It drew laughter in court when the informant, who was dressed as he was on the day of the incident, was indignant to the suggestion that his clothes were similar to those of the workmen, and so he had been mistaken for one of them and thus supplied with beer. The case against Mr Gibson was dismissed.

In 1938 plans were passed for alterations by the Cannon Brewery of Clerkenwell, London.

Belvoir Tavern - Station Road

*T*he Belvoir Tavern was purchased by Day, Noakes & Co. in 1865 the cost of the land was £260 and the building £800, suggesting a newly built property. It was well situated opposite Belvedere Railway Station through which it derived most of its trade. The landlord, Joseph Budd, applied in 1870 for a spirit licence having confidently just spent £200 on decorations and enlargements. He noted that thirty-one trains stopped on weekdays and thirty-eight on a Saturday and that some 4,000 persons passed up and down the street a week. He claimed that it was the nearest house to the actual station and thus should cater for

The Belvoir Tavern before demolition, early 1960's.

customers as though it were a Station Hotel similar to other establishments at Lewisham, Abbey Wood and Woolwich. His arguments were countered by the observation that where licensed houses were contiguous to the station they were often frequented by 'railway guards and others' who might better employ their time on the station. The spirit licence was refused and within six months Budd had moved to the Prince Alfred, Belvedere.

He was followed by a Mr Plummer, but only for a short while. At the licensing session for 1873 the bench were informed that a warrant was out for his arrest. He was accused of threatening behaviour and the police said he had fled to America though his wife pleaded that he had simply gone away on a business trip.

A plan of 1910 showed the pub to be an irregular shape internally as though it had been three buildings merged into one. At that time the bar parlour being removed to make a better serving area and the jug and bottle department was closed down. The counter had one six-pull and even a seven-pull beer engine. It was rebuilt in the 1960's.

Chequers/Crooked Billet - Picardy Road

Licences exist for a Crooked Billet from 1734 mentioning Richard Hickley. He is actually licensed in 1731 and 1733 but no pub sign is indicated. This pub may be on a site adjacent to the current one. James Barber ran the Crooked Billet until his death in 1852 and was succeeded by his son, Edmund, who renamed it the Chequers reusing the name of a pub that had stood on Belvedere Marshes.

The freehold of the pub was purchased in 1897 by brewers Kidds from Mrs F M Dashwood for £3,000, the pub having a full licence.

It was substantially rebuilt in 1907. Only the bar doors and windows to the left of the door and a small section of adjoining wall were retained, neatly incorporated in a building on a quite different orientation to the old. An unusual and novel feature was its large luncheon bar.

Though not as near as other pubs to the factories on the marshes with their large workforce of potential drinkers, the pub did a surprisingly high trade. The annual barrelage for some sample years was 1901 - 512, 1908 - 450, 1916 - 382 and 1918 (when other pubs had a little increase) a staggering 1,119.

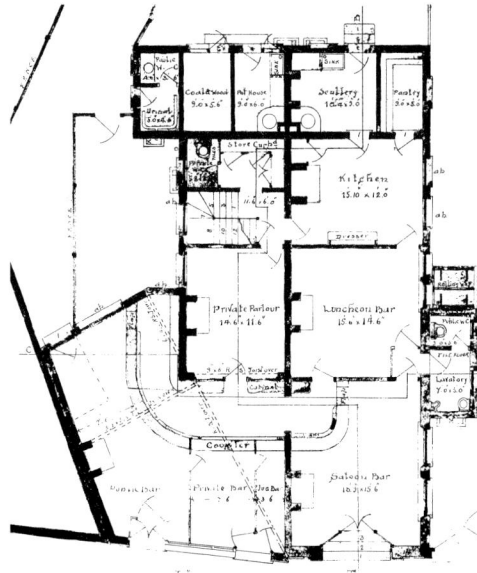

The Chequers, the proposed ground plan for the rebuilding. Previous internal walls are indicated by the dotted lines, 1907.

Eardley Arms - Woolwich Road

This is named after the Eardley family of Belvedere House the name of which supplanted the previous name for the district 'Lessness Heath' in the mid-19th century. The arms on the pub sign are a combination of those of Sampson Gideon junior (created Baron Eardley in 1789) and later members who married into his family.

The Eardley Arms from a rather crude but nonetheless detailed and attractive watercolour. An earlier illustration on which it was based is dated 1855.

The first licence was issued by 1801 but the pub may have been trading before 1789. Pigots Directory for 1829 unfortunately misspelt the pub as the Idlers Arms which I trust was not a reflection on its customers.

The lessees in the illustration, Coombe Delafield and Co., traded with that name until 1866, then becoming just Coombe & Co before merging with Watneys. The building illustrated is quite ancient with various additions over the years. It was rebuilt in the late 1860's and was acquired from the Eardley Trustees by Beasleys in 1879.

Fox - Nuxley Road

The present pub was refronted in 1921 altering buildings of 1853 for which the Deptford brewers, Norfolk & Sons, had obtained a ninety-nine year lease. The pub superseded in the early 1860's another 'Old Fox' beerhouse situated opposite. The licensed victualler of the Fox in 1861 was Jesse Stapley, who also farmed locally and after whom the adjacent road is named.

Halfway House - Lower Road

Lower Road was being developed in the 1860's and the Russell family, large landowners in the surrounding district, one of whom was the brewer from Gravesend, had for sale a thirty foot wide plot. James Bridge, then of the White Hart, Erith High Street, purchased it in October 1866 and built the pub and a cottage. He appears quite a speculator for he leased it in April 1867 to an Erith beerhouse keeper, Alfred Saunders, for twenty-one years at £40 p.a. On the basis of the security and income from the lease he raised an ambitious loan

The Fox, Upper Belvedere; a certificate of advancement through the Order of Odd Fellows given to William Wates at the Fox Tavern, Lessness Heath, 1862.

which he may have had difficulty repaying as in December 1867 he sold the pub to Alfred Saunders and moved from the White Hart to the Chequers at Picardy.

Saunders, on the other hand, prospered as he sold out to Beasleys in 1887 and with the proceeds erected a few yards away 1-3 Charles Cottages and on the opposite side of Lower Road, 3 and 4 Alfred Cottages.

The Halfway House, 1994.

Beasleys pulled down the pub and the cottage next door and erected the present structure in 1901. Their licensee, Alfred Wren, put in an application for a spirit licence which had been turned down in 1900 although another local house was granted one at that time on the surrender of a beer licence in the district. It was noted that ninety-eight houses had been erected opposite in the previous year. The local magistrates approved the application this year but it unfortunately was not confirmed by the county authorities. Wren kept applying because it was a condition of his lease (which included a clause requiring him to pay Beasleys a fee of £100 if successful) but the bench refused, saying that the population increase was insufficient reason.

Harrow - Abbey Road

A Harrow has been recorded as a pub for considerably longer than the present 1860's building. One is mentioned for 1715-1753 (though for 1734 John Little is described as at the Arrow) and Thomas Dennis was licensed from 1809-1820. It is also heard of in the 1830's.

In 1870 a court case involving George Fletcher, a blacksmith of Lessness-Heath, was reported under the heading of 'Dishonourable Borrower'. The Harrow, like many pubs, was the meeting place of various societies. George had borrowed £5 from the 'Friends of Labour Loan Society' and had only made six repayments of half a crown (12.5p) a week and nothing else for fifteen months. The secretary of the Society, a Henry West, who may have been related to the publican John West, was able to obtain a warrant of distress against Fletcher.

In 1928 when the Dartford Brewery built a new clubroom at the back of the grounds, their plans showed a bay fronted saloon fronting Knee Hill and an extension of a bar parlour to the south of that with a public bar (incorporating a bottle and jug servery) on the corner. By 1929 the bar parlour was described as a luncheon room and the garden bar as the lounge.

The Harrow , 1905.

The new owners, Style and Wynch, carried out further enlargements doubling the bar areas as the lounge became a private bar and the old saloon an enlarged bottle and jug, and a massive combined saloon and lounge was built to the rear. All the windows were restyled with slight baying within the wall thickness and insertion of decorative leaded lights. The ground floor facade was also tiled.

Leather Bottle - Heron Hill

*R*umour, but not evidence, says that there may have been a pub on this site back to the time of King Henry VIII. The core of the present building is said to date from 1643.

In 1783, when this was acquired by Taskers of Dartford, it was described as the Leather Bottle at Chalk-Stile. There is evidence for the building back to 1751 and the licences are recorded for a pub of this name back to 1726. The Leather Bottle was also a name given to a pub on the riverside.

The Leather Bottle, 1988.

Prince Alfred - Upper Abbey Road

*T*his is named after Queen Victoria's second son, Alfred, later Duke of Edinburgh, who was widely respected in the district after becoming

The Prince Alfred, 1994.

patron in 1866 of the Merchant Seaman's Institution at Belvedere House.

Henry Langman, a manager of one of the marsh powder magazines, signed a ninety-four and a half year lease in 1867 for newly built property on a quadrant of land adjacent to 4-27 Fairview Cottages. He initially employed a manager but later combined his then occupation of coopering next door with running the beershop himself. In 1887 he assigned his lease to Mitchell & Beasley of Plumstead. The freehold and ground rents of the pub and cottages were auctioned in 1899 and fetched £465. In 1899 the former cooperage was merged into

the pub in some extensive alterations which saw a long sweeping counter following the curve of the pub. Beasleys purchased the freehold shortly afterwards.

Prince of Wales - Woolwich Road

*T*he area in which the Prince of Wales was built, known as Lessness Heath, was common land until enclosed under an Act of Parliament in 1812. The recreation ground and open triangle in front of the pub are all that remains of the heath.

The pub's address was No 1 Alexandra Terrace and probably dates from 1863, the year the Prince of Wales, later King Edward VII, married Princess Alexandra of Denmark.

William James Seabrook applied for a spirit licence in 1870 but this was refused, despite his claims that the building had cost £2,000 to erect and that a further £600 had been spent on 'beautifying it'. Beasleys acquired the Prince of Wales in 1883.

The Prince of Wales, 1988.

Queens Head - Nuxley Road

*E*arlier versions of the Queens Head going back to at least the beginning of the 18th century lay at changing locations at the bottom of Nuxley Road, earlier called Bedonwell Hill.

The present Queens Head dates from around 1871. It was built by Thomas Mosebury Wyatt who ran it for twenty years before it passed to his son William. In 1901 William had entered into a contract to sell the house but before completion died suddenly.

The Queens Head's predecessor (from 1826-1870) at the junction of Bedonwell Road and Nuxley Road, c.1900.

In 1907 the licensee was reported for holding a lottery, as tickets and prizes of two rabbits and a goose had been seen on display. In fact, the actual draw was not to take place on the licensed premises but the secretary of a local friendly society, the 'Comical Fellows', had wished the pub to promote the sale of tickets which were to benefit the unemployed. He had sent the bird so that prospective patrons knew what they might win. The licensing bench disapproved and cautioned the publican.

Royal Standard - Nuxley Road

*T*his was founded by John Eves, a local market gardener, by 1862. He died in March 1867 and in his will left the business to his wife, Sarah, provided she didn't remarry. She continued to run the pub until the early 1870's and is still recorded as the owner in 1900.

The family frequently attracted the attention of the County Court. In 1870 her son John was in trouble for evading a warrant for several months. When the bailiffs arrived one summer morning they found him washing himself in the back yard. The bailiffs said that they allowed John to go upstairs to change into tidy clothes but were prevented from accompanying him by Mrs Eves who held them against the wall. The upstairs door was said to have been locked and John to have made his escape from a window. The under bailiff squeezed between his boss's legs to pass upstairs but was caught by Robert, another son, who struck him in the chest and barred his progress. Sarah, her daughter, said that her mother had invited the sub bailiff to dinner whilst her son dressed. She claimed her mother had a natural repugnance of other men scrambling up into her private rooms and that her brother Robert did nothing. The Eves also alleged that John did not escape but came down and found the bailiffs had left. The Eves were fined ten shillings each with costs and John Eves was later arrested.

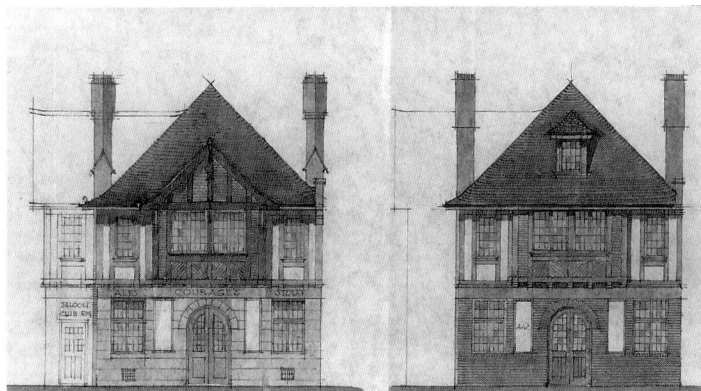

The Royal Standard, the front elevation proposals of 1929.

The pub suffered a fire in 1870 and Sarah was again taken to court in November and fined for not paying in full a Woolwich firm for a valuation and dilapidations report. She was again in court the following year, this time for selling beer after hours and for refusing to admit a police officer to the premises, for which she was fined forty shillings.

A later landlord, Edwin Tarr, was convicted in 1899 of selling adulterated whisky. In 1901, within the space of a fortnight, he was arrested and fined for being drunk on his own licensed premises and was quickly got rid of by the owners.

The pub was completely rebuilt in 1929 for its then owners, Courage. The brewery architect, F M Kirby, produced two delightful alternative proposals for the main front elevation to Bexley Road. One showed a two storey building with a dormer window in the attic and the other a simple plain gable. However, it was finally built as a three storied gable fronted building, with gentle Tudor arches capping the entrances and a battlemented side porch.

Victoria - Victoria Street

*T*his was in existence some time before 1869. It was one of the pubs the licensing authorities wanted to close down in 1906 under the 1904 Act because of its low sales and proximity to other pubs. The magistrates' decision was not backed up at the quarter sessions and the pub survived.

In 1925 the pub was enlarged by extending the club room and kitchen. An entrance was created in Albert Road leading into a tiny lobby, followed by the bottle and jug bar and finally a private room in which a new curved bar with a four pull beer engine was fitted.

The Victoria, 1977.

Northumberland Heath

Brewers Arms - Brook Street

*T*his was built by publican Thomas Neal in the mid-1860's but he later put in a manager. Trumans were the owners from 1876 whilst Neal lived next door and worked as a drayman.

A later tenant, Thomas Catlett, who ran the pub from 1870, conscientiously carried out a requirement in his lease to apply annually for a spirit licence. Although persistent he was consistently unsuccessful, his record causing laughter at his seventeenth refusal in 1891. A common clause in beerhouse-keepers' leases required them to apply for spirit licences, as once obtained they considerably improved the value of the property.

The Brewers Arms, 1977.

Duchess of Kent - Brook Street

George Heath, a local landowner, erected in the mid-19th century a terrace of three small cottages. The pub started off in the corner cottage and gradually took over the others.

In 1875 Crowleys of Croydon purchased the remaining thirteen years of a lease granted to James Chatwin who had moved to the Corner Pin in Slade Green. The price was £125 of which they paid £54 direct to Day Noakes & Co to clear Chatwin's mortgage and debts to them.

The pub at this time consisted of the centre

The Duchess of Kent, from plans of 1897.

cottage and the right hand cottage across the front of which a single storey extension had been erected. Internally was a tap room in the centre cottage with two bedrooms above, and a public bar with counter in the right hand cottage with club room above. There was a small private bar in the right hand part of the front extension.

This arrangement changed dramatically in 1897 to accommodate Northumberland Heath's rapidly expanding community. The remaining cottage was acquired and the brewers, Crowley's of Croydon, laid plans to raise the whole of the upper storey by three feet. The single storey front extension was built to full height making a spacious club room upstairs. This had a curved window capped by a pinnacled turret looking down Brook Street.

Downstairs had a bottle and jug department entered through a new door inserted into the right hand wall. One of the casualties of all this change was the removal of the pub sign post which had stood 40 feet away from the pub in the middle of the Sussex Road/Brook Street junction.

Not content with all this, in 1902 Crowley's extended the ground floor of what had been the left hand cottage thus forming a large saloon bar from what had been, for five years, the tap room. The bottle and jug department was moved to the front of the pub and the public bar spread over what had been the private bar.

Crowley's were fortunate in having a qualified architect, Reginald Crowley, in the family, producing one of the most attractive designs in the borough.

Duke of Northumberland - Bexley Road

*T*his pub was a speculative development by the Stoneham family in the mid-1860's and the first purpose built pub in Northumberland Heath. Its name is rather misleading as the Dukes of Northumberland have had no local associations. It is situated close to where the ancient parishes of Erith, Crayford and Bexley met.

It was planned as a fully licensed house and frequently attempted in its early years to obtain a spirit licence. It supported its claim in many ways, often by criticising aspects of the fully licensed Royal Oak. In 1870 the Odd Fellows friendly society presented a supporting petition and the police thought it was a well conducted house but this was countered by the comment that it was only surrounded by 300 inhabitants 'of the very poorest people that could possibly be found, and of the lowest class'!

In 1873 the applicants drew attention to the large capacity of the building and its good position to attract and deal with excursionists coming from London especially as "the immediate vicinity was of a very picturesque character".

A further unsuccessful claim in 1891 was backed by saying that the new railway line to be built from Erith to Bexleyheath (to which the Duke of Northumberland would be the nearest pub to the planned station at Northumberland Heath) would effectively make it the Railway Hotel and thus justify the sale of spirits.

They failed again in 1906, when their argument this time concerned the trams. The house stood where the Erith and Bexley tram lines terminated, and through journeys necessitated a change of cars. Passengers frequently had to wait up to twenty minutes as the trams' punctuality was not to be relied on. Consequently it was pleaded that there had been a further increase in the demand for spirits.

The Duke of Northumberland, c.1960.

Great Harry - Parsonage Manorway

*T*his is named after the flagship of Henry VIII's navy (and a maritime contemporary of the Mary Rose) the 'Great Harry' or 'Henri Grace a Dieu' built at Woolwich Dockyard and fitted out at Erith in 1514. The ship was accidently destroyed by fire at Woolwich in 1553.

Although plans were prepared and permission granted in 1947 it was to a design of 1950 that the pub was constructed.

The Great Harry, 1988.

Pheasant/Pages Arms - Belmont Road

*T*his was probably the earliest licensed house on the Heath, dating from the late 1830's. It was originally known as Pages Arms. The Pages were a local Erith landowning family, James Page Senior residing in a large old mansion which stood between West Street and the river where there now is a small public garden. The pub was renamed the Pheasant by 1861 though for the whole of the 1870's it appears to have reverted to its former name. Plans for the present pub, the third on the site, were passed in December 1935.

The Pheasant, Northumberland Heath, 1920's.

Royal Oak - Bexley Road

*T*he Royal Oak, created in the mid-1860's, had a full licence from its early years and thus was regarded jealously by the other beerhouses on the Heath. These were consistently refused full licences at sessions because they were too near to the Oak. In 1869 witnesses supporting the rival beerhouses were called to try to show the sale of 'inferior', and a year later, 'villainous' liquor. The Oak's landlord also drew custom by promoting competitive pedestrianism or long distance walking feats and races.

In November 1870 the licensee was fined forty shillings for Sunday trading. Police in plain clothes called at the back of the premises and on throwing a stone over a wall were asked by someone what they wanted. Replying a 'pot of beer' they were duly served. On hearing other conversation they looked over the fence to see men in a skittle alley with pots but in evidence could not say but only assume that they contained beer. They then went into the pub, had two further pints (which the court didn't think strictly necessary) where they found more people drinking but it was alleged that they were bona fide travellers and thus could legitimately be provided with drink.

The pub was entirely rebuilt by the Dartford Brewery Company in 1930. Central to the Bexley Road front was an outdoor department or off-licence. Recently this was merged with the bars either side and the curved bay window was removed. This has now found its way into our local museum collection.

The Royal Oak, decorated for George V's coronation in 1911.

Sidcup and The Crays

Albany - Steynton Avenue

*T*his was opened in April 1937. It was built in a style that is known as 'Brewers Tudor' to serve the growing estates of New Ideal Homesteads. It was strategically placed opposite the new railway station.

The Albany advertising its opening in April 1937.

Alma/Railway Tavern - Alma Road

*T*his was formerly known as the Railway Tavern and established in 1868. The pub retained its name, even when the Station Hotel was built, not changing to the Alma (from the road it stands in) until about 1970.

The first landlord, Henry Preston, was

The Alma as the Railway Tavern, c.1895.

wealthy enough to employ gamekeepers to look after a wood he occupied at the end of Birkbeck Road for shooting purposes. One day in September 1893, whilst out in the wood, they came upon the body of a Mr Kruse of Hadlow Road. After the police and a doctor were called they conveyed the corpse to the pub to await the Coroner's inquest. This inquest was held there two days later when death was said to have been caused by suffocation following a fit. Coroners' inquests were

commonly held in pubs but on this occasion Mr Booker, the foreman of the Coroner's jury, brought attention to the annoyance caused by keeping the body on the premises (can you hear the potman collecting glasses calling 'is that one dead?') and of the need for a public mortuary. Mr Cattar, the coroner, fully agreed, advising Mr Preston not to allow dead bodies on his premises again. He further ordered the police that on any future occasion to 'lay the corpse at the door of the Parish Overseer' as a means of speedily obtaining a proper mortuary.

In 1897 a billiard room, of almost the same floor area as the pub, was built for the then landlord, Mr Osborne. The pub also had, in addition to all the usual bars, a luncheon bar.

The next major rebuilding occurred in 1934 under Reffells ownership. They again engaged architect Kenneth Dalgliesh who had successfully worked for them on the rebuilding of the Woodman, Blackfen three years previously. The saloon bar was extended to one side into a small garden and on the other the tap room was extended. To the rear was an enlarged kitchen and dining room. The upper floor of this extension was covered in weatherboarding, a feature developed from Dalgliesh's work at the Woodman and similar to his commission at Old Forge Way off Rectory Lane, Sidcup also built in 1934.

Black Horse [Ye Olde] - Halfway Street

*L*icensing records of this Black Horse (which lay within the ancient parish of Bexley) go back to 1751 or possibly 1743. The rebuilt pub of 1892 has a date plaque of 1692 but this is unlikely to be accurate. The Crafter family owned and ran the pub from 1766 to 1849 when it became the property of Thomas Lewin of The Hollies opposite. Later (c 1877) a Colonel Beamish obtained from the Lewin estate the large house that stood on the site of the present British Telecom offices together with the Black Horse and numerous cottages in Halfway Street hamlet. Kidds then leased the pub and later demolished an adjacent pair of cottages. They built a new house for the land-lord and then the pub itself between February and May 1892.

The Black Horse, Halfway Street, showing the landlord's new house behind the yet to be demolished old pub, winter 1891.

Black Horse - High Street

*I*n 1703 Richard Manning of the Black Horse is recorded as Borsholder (or parish official) of Foots Cray. He is probably the same Richard

The Black Horse, Sidcup, 1897.

Manning who took out a licence in April 1692. The licences of the High Street Black Horse continue to 1791. It then became known as the Old Black Horse as Thomas Waller who took the pub in 1784 had another more modern pub built, which was, of course, called The New Black Horse! The two pubs continued until 1802 when the licence on the old ceased and the survivor was simply named the Black Horse. The pub known as Ye Olde Black Horse, Halfway Street is the newer by 100 years and the High Street Black Horse is really an Old Black Horse.

The 1855 directory records John Beacham at the Black Horse Inn, Tea Gardens and Cricket Ground. It was clearly a large establishment as confirmed by the 1861 census which records as living-in employees a barmaid, housemaid, cook, ostler, waiter and an 'oddman'.

A later landlord tried unsuccessfully in 1871 to get a music and dancing licence for Masonic balls but a year later he was granted permission to open from 5 am to 12 midnight for the accommodation of persons going to and from the London markets.

In 1893 the old skittle alley was partly converted into a coffee room accessed from the private bar. Above it was a large dining room with a small retiring room for the hotel guests. The remainder was demolished as was half the stable block and built in its place was a billiard room with large club room above.

Charcoal Burner - Main Road

*T*his was built in 1960 on the site of an imposing late Victorian villa known as 'The Croft'.

The Charcoal Burner, 1994.

Russet brown sand faced tiling.

2" Dorking fac Bricks - Light multi colour

D.º D.º Dark- multi colour

ELEVATION TO SIDCUP ROAD.

The Horse and Groom as never built, from plans submitted for the rebuilding due to have taken place in 1939.

Horse and Groom - Main Road

*T*his is situated in a area that was known as Pound Place, a leftover segment from road improvements made by The New Cross Turnpike Trust during the mid-1790's. The pub was founded by 1847 by the enterprising young widow, Eliza Shaw, to provide for her family. She, and her husband George, an agricultural labourer (and possibly a groom) lived on the site in previous years. She is additionally described as tea dealer in 1869. She continued to run the pub until the mid-1880's assisted over the last twenty years by her sister Charlotte. By 1899 it was in the hands of

Bromley Common brewers, Jones & Veness, who had a large games room erected on the east side of the building.

Whitbreads, who had leased it from 1901, purchased its freehold and that of an adjoining property in 1939 and prepared plans for a complete rebuilding. The new house was to have been of three storeys with a hipped roof and dormers in the upper floor. It was to have art deco styled iron window frames including a superb two storey window at the rear. Due to the war it was never built.

The old pub was damaged during the war and a temporary hut set up. This lasted until the arrival of the present building, opened on Armistice Day 1960.

69

Iron Horse/Station Hotel - Station Road

*T*he Station Hotel, built by local developer G Hawkins at a cost of £2,500, opened in July 1879. It was well placed to serve this function and had the endorsement of the railway company, a status enhanced by the alleged unsuitability of the Old Black Horse and the Alma. Despite this, and large scale housing developments nearby (financed by Hawkins on land owned by Mr Malcolm of Lamorbey), it had great difficulty in obtaining a licence. The application was opposed by nearby residents some of whom had been induced to sign a petition stating that 'the house would be a resort of

The Station Hotel. An interior of the sumptuous dining room decorated by an elaborate tapestry above the dresser, 1954.

pigeon shooters and loose characters'. The licence was granted in 1880 and William Thompson Wyatt, the tenant, quickly sold his lease in 1881 to Beasleys of Plumstead.

This fine hotel was demolished and a new pub opened on 31st October 1976 by constituency MP Sir Edward Heath. In plans of 1972 the new pub was originally destined to be called The Horse Brass but the alternative metal and name of the Iron Horse was agreed on; a much more appropriate name for a pub adjacent to a railway.

Red Lion - High Street, Footscray

*T*his stands on Footscray High Street, the main turnpike road to Maidstone. A Red Lion is mentioned in Chislehurst in 1705 (the parish in which this part of the High Street lay) but is not this establishment. The Foots Cray Red Lion originates with the Murrell family who ran it 1726-52.

In the 1840's George Eagles Marsden, a Lewisham brewer, owned it and Whitbreads took over from his successors in 1891.

Whitbreads undertook major works in 1938 when the shop next door (to the west) was taken over and the dividing wall demolished to make larger bar space. At the same time they created a wonderful ground floor facade.

In 1972 the Council placed a Compulsory Purchase Order on the Red Lion as the site was required for housing development. Whitbreads vigorously opposed the order and to the delight of the local inhabitants were successful in their appeal to the Secretary of State for the Environment.

The eastern end of the pub building incorporates part of a large medieval structure (which had become subdivided over time) which formed the body of the Village Stores next door. This was discovered when the those premises were investigated by archaeologists during its demolition in 1981/82. The stores building was constructed in four main phases and the earliest was that part which became shared with the pub. The archaeologists' plan shows a single timber bay within the pub but plans of the alterations made in 1938 show evidence of two ten foot bays. The second was destroyed or hidden at this time when Whitbreads converted the dining room into a lounge. Careful investigation of the roof space and upper floor would clarify development of the complex architectural history and repay the effort involved.

Seven Stars/Plough - High Street, Footscray

*T*he Seven Stars is the other surviving pub in Foots Cray. It is in an attractive weatherboarded building that protrudes alarmingly onto the road. The timber framed section of the building (at right angles to the road) dates from the 16th century.

There is some uncertainty as to the origin of its name. The seven stars are currently depicted surrounding the Virgin Mary's head, and this religious reference is supported by the discovery of a carving of the Virgin's head with stars found in the pub's well. This was probably a corbel removed from All Saints Church during the Reformation. It is now set into the bar wall. The more likely origin is a little more prosaic as the pub had previously been

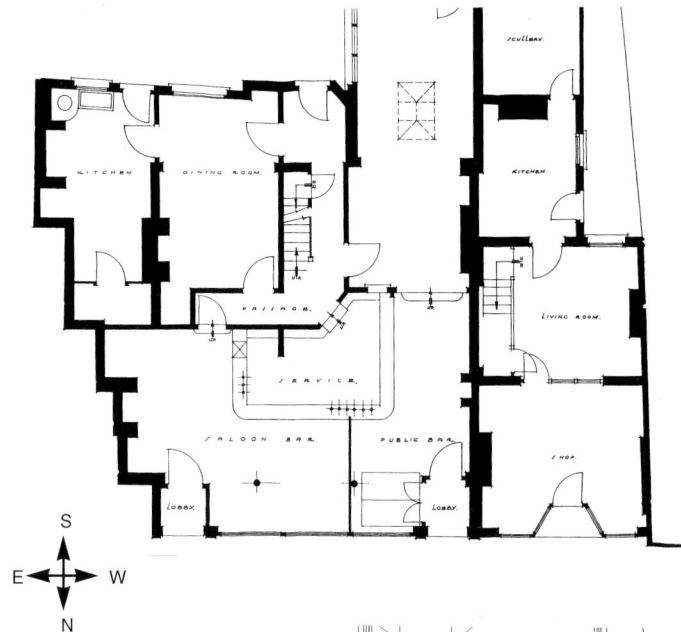

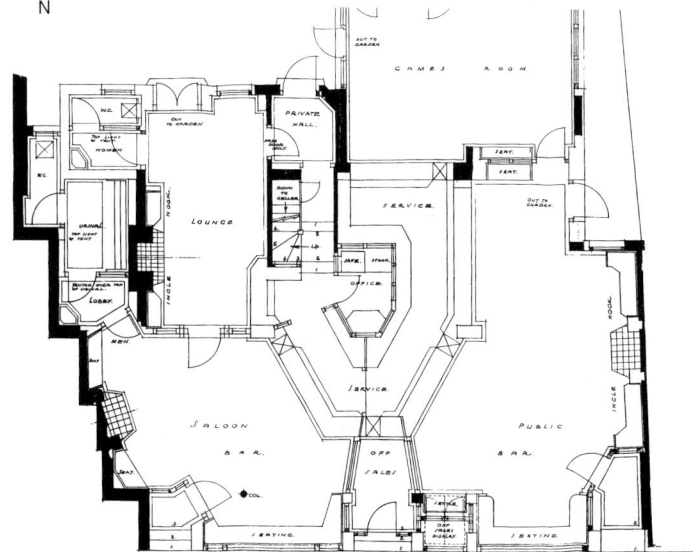

The Red Lion, Footscray; plans of 1938, before alterations (top) and after (bottom). The former kitchen and dining room are the two medieval bays .

called the Plough and the inn sign depicted not the agricultural implement but the seven-starred constellation.

In 1717 Richard Peake is licensed at the Chequers, Foots Cray. In 1718 and 1723 he is recorded at 'The Plow'. Its name was changed to the present one by his widow some time between 1736 and 1751. Following her it was

The Seven Stars, a drawing by Irons, of 1947 based on an earlier illustration of c.1900.

run from time to time between 1760 and 1850 by generations of the Edmunds families.

Its importance in the village is confirmed by its position from the 1820's as the posting house.

In 1912 when brewers Hoare & Co replaced the timber wing parallel to the road they inadvertently infringed building regulations and were successfully prosecuted by Foots Cray Urban District Council.

White Cross/Red Cross - North Cray Road

*E*vidence concerning the White Cross dates back to 1729 when William Jones is recorded at Ye Brandy Shop and Alehouse, North Cray. From 1730 it is called the Red Cross. Hussey Fleet, Brewers of Dartford, acquired the property in 1820.

In 1935 the War Office ruled that the pub name contravened the Geneva Convention as it made an inappropriate reference to the Red Cross Society. Accordingly the brewers changed colour to White. At present the inn sign depicts a white Maltese Cross - the sign of the Knights Hospitallers and by derivation also of the St John's Ambulance Brigade. I hope they are not required to change it again - Blue Cross may have animal rights campaigners upset and Green Cross for road safety.

The White Cross, the change in the colour of the cross from Red to White, 1935.

East Wickham and Welling

Duchess of Edinburgh/The Fighting Cocks - Upper Wickham Lane

*T*his was founded in the mid 1850's reviving an earlier name as pubs called the Fighting Cock, The Two Fighting Cocks and the Old Fighting Cocks had been in East Wickham until the later 18th century.

In 1874 landlord, Mr Wren, applied for a spirit licence noting the pub's position on the four-times daily horse bus route to Woolwich and visiting pleasure parties. He emphasised the better conducted business brought about by the change of pub's name which had been occasioned by the marriage at the beginning of that year between Marie, daughter of Alexander II of Russia and Queen Victoria's son, Alfred Duke of Edinburgh. Unlike many applications at this time it found favour with the magistrates and was successful. The present building dates from 1937.

The old Duchess of Edinburgh 1934.

Fanny on the Hill/White Horse - Wickham Street

*A*n enduring story concerns this pub's association with Shooters Hill highwaymen and Dick Turpin in particular to whom the landlady would signal the approach of likely prey. No documentary evidence supports this and the problem of highwaymen had all but disappeared at the time of the pub's establishment.

The original White Horse beerhouse lay in an area known as Hill(y) Grove or sometimes Chalks on a footpath between the present pub

The old Fanny on the Hill, 1951.

and the Foresters Arms. The first recorded landlord seems to be Thomas Tyler shown in a directory of 1847. He was succeeded by Anne Muirhead (most likely the original 'Fanny') who ran the pub for around 20 years in the mid 19th century.

Anne Muirhead and later landlords attempted to take advantage of the pub's isolated position by tolerating drunken behaviour and extended hours. She had been fined on numerous occasions and in 1897 the landlord John Bond and three others were discovered drinking after hours. They were locals but falsely claimed to be travellers from Silvertown and could therefore legitimately be served. All were convicted and fined.

Beasleys purchased the pub from Bond in 1927. Although they had permission for the removal of the licence in 1949 they did not rebuild the pub on the edge of Wickham Street until 1957.

The pub's nickname was so strong that at various times it has been painted in larger letters than the pub name and a few years ago it officially supplanted 'The White Horse'.

Foresters Arms - Wickham Lane

*T*his was built around 1860 by William Dawson alongside three cottages he had built five years previously. Dawson, and also brewer

A token from the Foresters Arms.

Lewis Davis to whom it was leased, had links with the local brickmaking industry and the pub's address is sometimes given as New Brickfields.

The pub was 'improved' and had a date stone 1874 with M & B (standing for Mitchell & Beasley - successors to Davis) inserted at the top of the facade, though unfortunately on a more recent 'improvement' this was obscured.

John M Corkett, who was licensee from 1889, issued a 4d. token. The manufacturer made a Cockett by mis-spelling the landlord's name but examples seen by the author have been carefully countermarked with an 'R'. John was succeeded in 1900 by his widow Bessie who ran it until 1916.

Glenmore Arms - Glenmore Road

*T*his was a new pub in 1939 but not a new licence. Beasleys had owned since 1874 a pub on Plumstead Common Road called the Barnfield Arms. That was shut and the licence removed to the East Wickham pub. Glenmore Road at one time was known as Blind Lane.

The Glenmore Arms, 1994.

The Foresters Arms, a busy scene looking north along the footpath from the Fanny on the Hill on Wickham Street to Wickham Lane. Plumstead Cemetery is in the background, c.1900.

Green Man - Wickham Street

*T*his was part of a development on five acres of land leased in 1868 from Edward Hobday of Woodlands Farm, Welling to the Plumstead builder Joseph Lidbetter. Lidbetter was required to build by the end of that September 'one messuage shop and dwelling intended as a beerhouse of the third rate or class of the value of not less than £600'. Under the agreement two shops were planned by 1869 and twelve cottages (of the fourth rate) by 1875. However, it appears that the shops and one of the cottages were never erected.

Beasleys acquired the pub in 1875 and rebuilt it between 1937 and 1939.

The old Green Man, c.1930

Guy Earl of Warwick - Park View Road

*T*he old pub stood west of the present building on part of the site of John Newton Court. Licences for it can be traced back to Richard Ebbs in 1730. The pub was greatly enlarged in 1792 when the range that lay alongside the road was erected in front of an earlier structure. Adjacent to this pub was the equally ancient Hope Lodge which became a private school. When that moved at the turn of the century the buildings and pleasure gardens were merged with the pub. Kidds of Dartford purchased the pub from Ann Bean of Danson Mansion in 1895 at a cost of £5,000.

Dickens, in 'Great Expectations', mentions the Guy but renamed it as the 'Halfway House' (halfway between London and Gravesend) where Pip stopped on his last visit to Miss Havisham before travelling on to Rochester.

When the old pub was demolished a passage was discovered which led up to a secret space between the attics above and rooms below. There was speculation that this was used either as a place to hide from naval press gangs or, with the landlord's connivance, for highwaymen to spy upon the occupants of the rooms below to select suitable wealthy persons to rob.

The new pub was opened for business on 11th August 1926. Locals may note a narrow crossover on the Roseacre Road frontage. This was to allow drivers of 89 and 160 buses to skilfully draw up alongside the pub when terminating there.

During preliminary work on the building of McKinlay Court on part of the pub's extensive garden, evidence of Roman activity was discovered. The Kent Archaeological Rescue

Unit conducted an emergency dig in which the author assisted. It was of great importance as it proved for the first time that a part of Welling was intensively covered by Roman features during the whole of their 400 year occupation. Evidence of enclosures and a small hut with tiled hearth, wooden lined wells and a small cemetery of five cremation burials were amongst the discoveries. No evidence of a Roman taverna was found on the site!

Lord Kitchener - Wrotham Road

This was approved in 1937 and completed in January 1939. Named after the famous Field Marshal, hero of the Sudan and South Africa, his was the face and pointing finger in the 1916 poster demanding 'Your Country Needs You'.

The Lord Kitchener, 1951.

The Guy Earl of Warwick c.1907.

Moon & Sixpence/Station Hotel - Bellegrove Road

In May 1895 the Bexleyheath Railway was opened. Application was made in 1896 to remove the licence from an old established Welling pub to new premises to be called the Railway Hotel. Application was, of course, opposed by solicitors acting for the Plough &

The Station Hotel, later the Moon and Sixpence, c.1925.

Harrow beerhouse opposite. Amongst his complaints was that with only six bedrooms (most of which would be filled by the land-lord's family) it hardly deserved to be called a 'hotel' erected for the public benefit, but was merely speculative. However, after alterations which doubled the Dover Road frontage to 100 feet, increased the bedrooms to nine and reduced the entrances from seven to five, the revised application was granted. The pub was

erected the following year and was a most attractive design though unfortunately the lovely brick and terracotta work has been recently overpainted.

After becoming a 'trendy' disco pub in 1970 whose long hours and noisy clientele distressed the local community, the pub has recently undergone a £300,000 refurbishment and has been renamed the Moon and Sixpence.

The author's family told him that this pub was always known as "the Palm Court" because of the landlady's fondness for so decorating the interior. In contrast the Plough & Harrow opposite was always just "the beerhouse".

Nags Head/Nags Head and Punch Bowl - High Street

*T*he first recorded landlord is Thomas Richards. In 1743 he is licensed for the Nags Head & Punch Bowl and later, 1751-56, his pub is simply described as the Nags Head. The following licensee, Thomas Keeble or Kibble was replaced by George Fell in 1819.

The freehold was acquired by publican Evelyn Saunders in 1850 and he ran it for about ten years before letting it to Day, Noakes & Son. His executors put it (and the Rose and Crown) up for auction in 1891. The Nags Head was described as having a 'Modern liquor shop and private bar, fitted with a plate glass front, large commercial room, tap room and capital bar parlour'. The extensive grounds included a large weather-boarded dining saloon, two boarded summer houses, a bowling green and a brick and slate skittle ground.

There was also a large kitchen garden, pigeon house, range of piggeries and even a duck pond. It was purchased by Mrs Talfourd Hughes for £1,120. Nearby Springfield Road was formerly called Talfourd Road.

The present building was erected before the last war.

The old Nags Head. Harman was the landlord from 1868 until he died in 1871.

Plough & Harrow - Bellegrove Road

*I*n the 1830's the area between Westwood Lane and what is now Kelvin Road was being developed and by 1840 the Plough Beer Shop was established.

Kidds of Dartford purchased the lease in 1875 and seven years later the freehold. Their property register notes that it formerly consisted of "the beerhouse and a cottage but the two have been since thrown together". Much later they purchased the shop next door in

The Plough and Harrow shortly before its rebuilding, c.1934.

readiness for expansion and local builder, Ellinghams, were engaged to rebuild the pub in 1935 at a cost of £4,525.

In 1872 landlord Silas Durling innocently infringed closing time which had been changed at the introduction of the Licensing Act of that year. A fortnight after its passing he was summoned for having his house open for the sale of liquor at 10.45 pm on a Sunday. Part of his defence was that the police had called to advise him that the new Act would not alter his opening hours. The police claimed that their message was only about weekdays and not Sundays and that they had no instructions to say anything about Sunday hours. The solicitor in court commented that some experienced officers were uncertain as to the requirements of the new Act. The Chairman of the bench thought Sunday closing should be 10 pm but even Police Inspector Butt thought that it might be 11 pm because the population of the district was over 2,500. The police confirmed that Durling appeared to have no notion that he was acting illegally and immediately closed on being told of the correct situation. In the circumstances the bench dismissed the case. The five accused customers also had their summons for 'misdemeanours' quashed. Many aspects of the 1872 Act were difficult to interpret and within two years a supplementary act was passed which altered the hours of opening and closing again.

Rose and Crown - Welling High Street

*T*he earliest reference to the Rose and Crown is a Richard Hill licensed in 1751, though records for the site go back to 1694. It lay within three acres of cherry orchard. The early documents reveal some delightful names as in 1775 when Neighbour Frith, a London silk weaver, leased the pub to a Street Holding.

Descendants of Frith leased the pub in 1808 for £1,130 to Paul Greathead, a victualler from Carnaby Street, London. He obtained a mortgage of £500 from William Clarke, a brewer of Bermondsey, and no doubt had to sell his beer. Though Bermondsey may seem a long way away to deliver over the roads of the time the water there was suitable for brewing the popular London Porter. A successor to Clarke was Day Noakes & Co who held pubs in the area and who also brewed pale beers at their Westerham brewery.

The pub was burnt down in the 1870's. A former member of the Bexleyheath Fire Brigade recalled in 1938 of being on duty that evening. This local brigade, which had only been formed in 1869, kept their engine at Mr Moody's at Bexleyheath Market Place. When the midnight call came there was great difficulty in obtaining horses to pull the engine. Eventually they persuaded Charles Mansfield to hitch up two of his omnibus horses and they set off for Welling. They arrived about 1 am to loud boos of the assembled crowd, as the pub was by then destroyed and the fire was spreading to adjacent Mitchell's bakery. They suffered further indignity by being beaten to the fire hydrant by members of the Shooters Hill Brigade. Shamefaced they remounted their engine and returned to Bexleyheath vowing to ensure that horses were always ready on call.

The rebuilt pub was sold at auction in 1891 by the descendants of Evelyn Saunders who had been owner occupier of the Nags Head. It contained a tap room, bar, parlour, bar parlour with a clubroom upstairs, whilst in the garden was a skittle ground.

The Rose and Crown, Welling High Street, before the building was destroyed by fire; Morris was landlord from 1867 to October 1872.

We Anchor in Hope - Bellegrove Road

*T*he speculation that this pub dates back to the early 1700's is unfounded. The source of this inaccuracy is an Anchor in Hope noted in Blackheath licensing returns which, in fact, relates to a pub in Erith. The location at the bottom of Shooters Hill is ideal for a pub but from 1800 East Wickham had just two pubs, the Nags Head and the Rose and Crown.

This pub started up as a consequence of the 1830 Beerhouse Act and the first publican noted in a directory of 1832 is George Finch.

He was succeeded by his daughter in 1857 followed soon after by John Dorrington, a cattle dealer, who had been a lodger in the pub for twenty years.

The present building appears to date from the mid-1850's and has a fine pair of chimney stacks. The single storey right hand wing, once the stables, was damaged in the war and later rebuilt with a flat roof though the outline of the hipped roof of the original can still be clearly seen on the flank wall of the main part of the pub.

The We Anchor in Hope, 1951.

Appendix I

List of Sources Consulted

Bexley Local Studies Centre

Directories 1792 - 1939
Census Returns 1841 - 1891
Rate Books
Newspapers
Tithe Maps and Schedules
Planning Records
Manorial Records
Land and Window Taxes
Parish Registers
Deeds
Wills

Centre for Kentish Studies

Records of licensed victuallers 1646-1827
Land Tax Returns
Deeds
Wills

Greater London Record Office

Records of Trumans Brewery
Records of companies taken over
by Courage

Courage Archives

Deeds
Property Ledgers
Tenant Change Book

Charrington's Archives

Deeds

Greenwich Local History Library

Records of Blackheath Petty Sessions
Directories 1792 - 1900

Dartford Central Library

Newspapers

C 716

(No. 199. *Retail Beer, Ale, Cyder, and Perry Licence.*)

№ *367*   №

G R

WE, whose Names are hereunto subscribed and Seals set, being the Collector of Excise of *Rochester* Collection, and the Supervisor of Excise of *Dartford* District, within the said Collection, in pursuance of an Act of Parliament made in the Forty-eighth Year of the Reign of His late Majesty King George the Third, do hereby authorize *Richard Webb* being an Alehouse Keeper, residing in a House known by the Sign of *Blackbirds* in the Parish of *Bexley, Blendon* within the said Collection, to sell Beer or Ale by Retail, and also Cyder, and Perry, to be drank or consumed in the said House and Premises thereunto belonging, and not elsewhere, from the Time of the granting of this Licence until and upon the Tenth Day of *October* next ensuing, he having paid *£ 2 .. 2 .. 0* for this Licence to the said Collector of Excise. Given under our Hands and Seals this *Thirtieth* Day of *October* in the *Second* Year of the Reign of our Sovereign Lord George the Fourth, by the Grace of God, of the United Kingdom of Great Britain and Ireland, King, Defender of the Faith, and in the Year of our Lord 18 *21*

Seaton   Collector

James   Supervisor

A licence of 1821 for the Three Blackbirds, Blendon

Appendix II

Sources and their hazards

The bulk of this work is derived from research using primary records.

I started with directories which date from 1792. County directories, published every few years, contain classified lists of persons in trade and commerce as well as the nobility and gentry, usually by parish though later ones reflected the growth of certain districts by allocating them their own section. Local directories available from 1890 are often arranged by street, noting occupiers under their address followed by an alphabetically arranged listing by surname. Regarding pubs, the custom was to list those with full licences by the pub name and then by the publican. Those with only a beer licence were listed by licensee followed by the designation, beer retailer or beerhouse keeper (but no sign) which makes it difficult to trace the origins of some of our local establishments.

Use of the decennial census helped clarify some of the problems generated by the directories but again these do not necessarily name the pub. They reveal in the 19th century that some publicans would be away in the daytime carrying out another trade, only sharing the running of the pub in the evening. Though house numbers were not in general use one could sometimes work out the location of a beerhouse in relation to other known points. An aid to this is the use of Tithe Maps.

Under an Act of 1836 the tax or 'tithe' that people paid, often in the form of every tenth lamb or tenth bushel of corn etc., could be commuted into an annual cash sum. To this end maps of parishes were drawn up depicting and numbering the fields and buildings. Attached to this was a schedule detailing the landowner and the majority of the occupiers of each plot, together with a land/property description which for some would note 'public house' and occasionally the actual name.

These lead onto the wonderful large scale Ordnance Survey maps where in the first edition of the 1860's some buildings were marked PH/BH for Public/Beer House. Unfortunately in one or two cases this otherwise impeccable source seems to have noted the wrong building.

A major source for early years are the records of licensed victuallers, held at the Centre for Kentish Studies at Maidstone. Though commencing in 1659 (for other areas 1646) the half dozen or so records surviving from before 1700 do not mention pub names. The rolls (of animal skin), about 20 in number falling intermittently within the next fifty years, do for the most part link names and publicans. There is a fine bound annual series commencing with a change of licensing law in 1753 and ceasing in 1827, which, apart from a couple of years, regrettably does not indicate pub signs. Their use is not always straightforward. For example, a new licensee recorded the same year that another appears to cease does not necessarily indicate continuity. It may

List of publicans for good faith, 1850, from the churchwardens' account book of St. Mary's, Bexley.

show the closure of one pub and the opening of another in a completely different area of the parish. A licensee recorded continuously for ten years does not, as I have found, mean that he was at the same pub. The mention of a Bull in 1700 and 1800 does not necessarily mean it is the same pub or even the same site. Modern local licensing records apparently only note whether a pub was established before the 1869 Act and not when it was founded.

Rate books recording the assessment and payment of property rates to the parish are a good source but whilst the earliest Crayford survivor is over 250 years old there are frustrating gaps after 1882. Bexley rate books date back to 1790 and East Wickham to the 1870's though there are a couple for the late 1850's. Erith lost thirty odd years worth when the Church was being restored in 1877 and the temporary wooden church that they were stored in was destroyed by fire. Amongst the Erith Tithe Commissioners papers was a note that earlier records were said to have been destroyed by a former rate collector who went mad. This has made research particularly difficult concerning the start of North Heath pubs.

Rate books before 1900 rarely mention beerhouses by sign and not always whether a building is anything other than a house or shop. It is not normal for rate books prior to 1836 to even distinguish whether the charge is for land or buildings. Clues of pubs starting and closing can come by noting from the rate book whether all the rates due were received by the collector, or if a reason was given for any abatement.

Hearth Tax returns of the 17th century (some of which I have transcribed) and which list personal names against number of fire-places, are useful for comparing sizes of licensed premises. Unfortunately they relate to a period where we have little confirmation of continuity of pubs to present times.

Similarly, records of the 18th century Window Tax (you think you are widely taxed now!) do not link taxpayers with named establishments. The Land Tax returns from 1762 to 1832 have proved useful in indicating brewery owners/lessees of various pubs. However its records of ownership and occupier were not regularly updated.

Property deeds are very useful for public houses but again in the 19th century beer-houses' signs are rarely mentioned. Survival and location of deeds is a considerable problem, breweries often do not have full sets and currently with pubs being sold from brewers, deeds are being dispersed. Legal affidavits should be treated with caution as the reason they were made can sometimes influence their contents. One relating to the Prince Alfred, Upper Abbey Road (formerly Leather Bottle Lane) claimed that it was once known as the 'Leather Bottle beerhouse' a fact not substantiated anywhere else. Another claimed that the Duchess of Kent, Northumberland Heath originally consisted of four cottages rather than three but this appears a device to disguise an error in an earlier deed.

Plans of pubs are very useful showing the arrangements of bars and fittings. Though Bexley Local Studies Centre has a considerable number from the 1880's onwards the where-abouts of those of some areas of the Borough are unknown. In Victorian times local builders would often draw up the plans and upon approval by the client execute them. For later periods professional architects took over and C B Mears has produced a useful study of his relatives, J O Cooke Snr and Jnr, whose practise did the majority of the work required by Beasleys, brewers of Plumstead. Kenneth Dalgliesh was similarly engaged on commissions for Reffells of Bexley but much more research awaits the architectural historian. Plans should however be treated with some caution since there were often amendments carried out on site during construction or alteration.

Newspaper reports should always be treated with care. I wasted time investigating a non-existent Belvedere pub of 1878 by the station. The 'Railway Tavern 100 yards from the Belvoir' should have read the 'Belvoir 100 yards from the Belvedere Hotel'. Reports from the annual licensing sessions reveal that publicans quoting how long their establishment had been open is often guesswork or exaggeration.

other

Flour

tatoes

sour

rtern

nberland

:RITH.

892.

CROSS KEYS HOTEL,

ERITH, KENT.

W. B. SMITH.

(neo KATE HARVEY.)

THIS old historic, well-known tavern, has been entirely re-built, and contains every modern improvement. Splendid accommodation; unrivalled river views from balconies and terrace; noble dining and concert room, overlooking magnificent river prospect; bedrooms, bathroom, &c., &c.

MRS. W. B. SMITH

in thanking her many friends and supporters for past favours, begs to draw their attention to the fact that she has now opened her new house, and hopes with the increased facilities at her command, to merit a continuance of their good will.

Special facilities for Yachting Parties.

Luncheons, Dinners, Teas, &c., to order.

Cold Luncheons, Chops, Steaks, &c., on the shortest notice.

Commercial Luncheons.

Wines, Spirits, Malt Liquors, Cigars, &c., of the choicest description.

Clubs accommodated. Picnic Parties, Beanfeast Parties, &c., specially catered for.

ESTIMATES GIVEN.

RE-OPENING DAY,

BANK HOLIDAY, MONDAY, AUGUST 1st

Music and Dancing on the Platform, and

Don't you forget it!!

Advertisement for the rebuilt Cross Keys, Erith, from the Erith Times 1892. The previous building had been destroyed by fire (see page 41).

Appendix III

Bibliography

Cockes, Bernard Walter **Three centuries: the story of our ancient brewery, Barclay, Perkins & Co. Ltd.** Harley Publishing Co., 1951.

Strong, L. A. G. **A brewer's progress 1757-1957 A survey of Charrington's Brewery on the occasion of its bicentenary** Charringtons, 1957.

Janes, Hurford **The red barrel: a history of Watney Mann** Murray, 1963.

The story of Whitbread's Whitbread and Co., 1964.

Monckton, Herbert Anthony **A history of the English public house** Bodley Head, 1969.

Osborne, Keith **Bygone breweries** Rochester Press, 1982.

Clark, Peter **The English alehouse: a social history, 1200-1830** Longman, 1983.

Girouard, Mark **Victorian pubs** Yale University Press, 1984.

Hackwood, F. W. **Inns, ales and drinking customs of old England** Bracken Books, 1985.

Mirams, Michael David **Kent inns and signs** Meresborough Books, 1987.

Baker, Chris and Hinkley, Graham **Cheers! A hundred years, a hundred Dartford pubs** Dartford Borough Council, 1990.

Richmond, Lesley and Turton, Alison (Eds.) **The brewery industry - a guide to historical records** Manchester University Press, 1990.

Hayes, Ralph **Hotel and pub checks of Greater London** R Hayes c.1991.

Mears, C. B. **J.O. Cook & Son architects and surveyors, Woolwich** Typescript, 1991.

Moynihan, Peter and Goodley, Ken **A brief history of the Black Eagle Brewery Westerham** Brewery History Society, 1991.

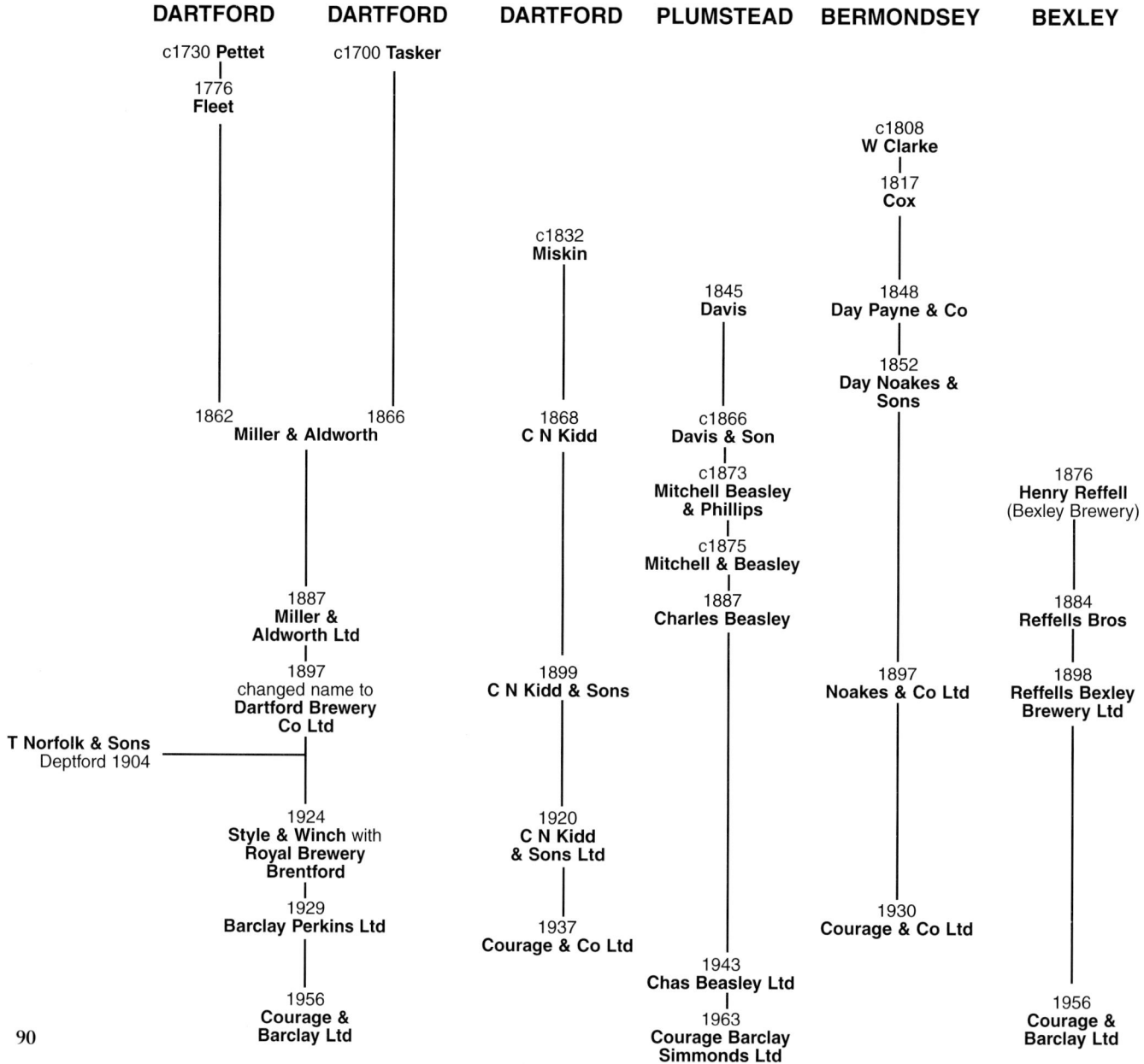

DARTFORD	DARTFORD	DARTFORD	PLUMSTEAD	BERMONDSEY	BEXLEY

c1730 **Pettet**

c1700 **Tasker**

1776
Fleet

c1808
W Clarke

1817
Cox

c1832
Miskin

1845
Davis

1848
Day Payne & Co

1852
Day Noakes & Sons

1862   1866
Miller & Aldworth

1868
C N Kidd

c1866
Davis & Son

c1873
Mitchell Beasley & Phillips

1876
Henry Reffell
(Bexley Brewery)

c1875
Mitchell & Beasley

1887
Miller & Aldworth Ltd

1887
Charles Beasley

1884
Reffells Bros

1897
changed name to
Dartford Brewery Co Ltd

1899
C N Kidd & Sons

1897
Noakes & Co Ltd

1898
Reffells Bexley Brewery Ltd

T Norfolk & Sons
Deptford 1904

1924
Style & Winch with
Royal Brewery Brentford

1920
C N Kidd & Sons Ltd

1929
Barclay Perkins Ltd

1937
Courage & Co Ltd

1930
Courage & Co Ltd

1943
Chas Beasley Ltd

1956
Courage & Barclay Ltd

1963
Courage Barclay Simmonds Ltd

1956
Courage & Barclay Ltd

A Brewery 'Family Tree' showing the absorption of breweries mentioned into the main combines

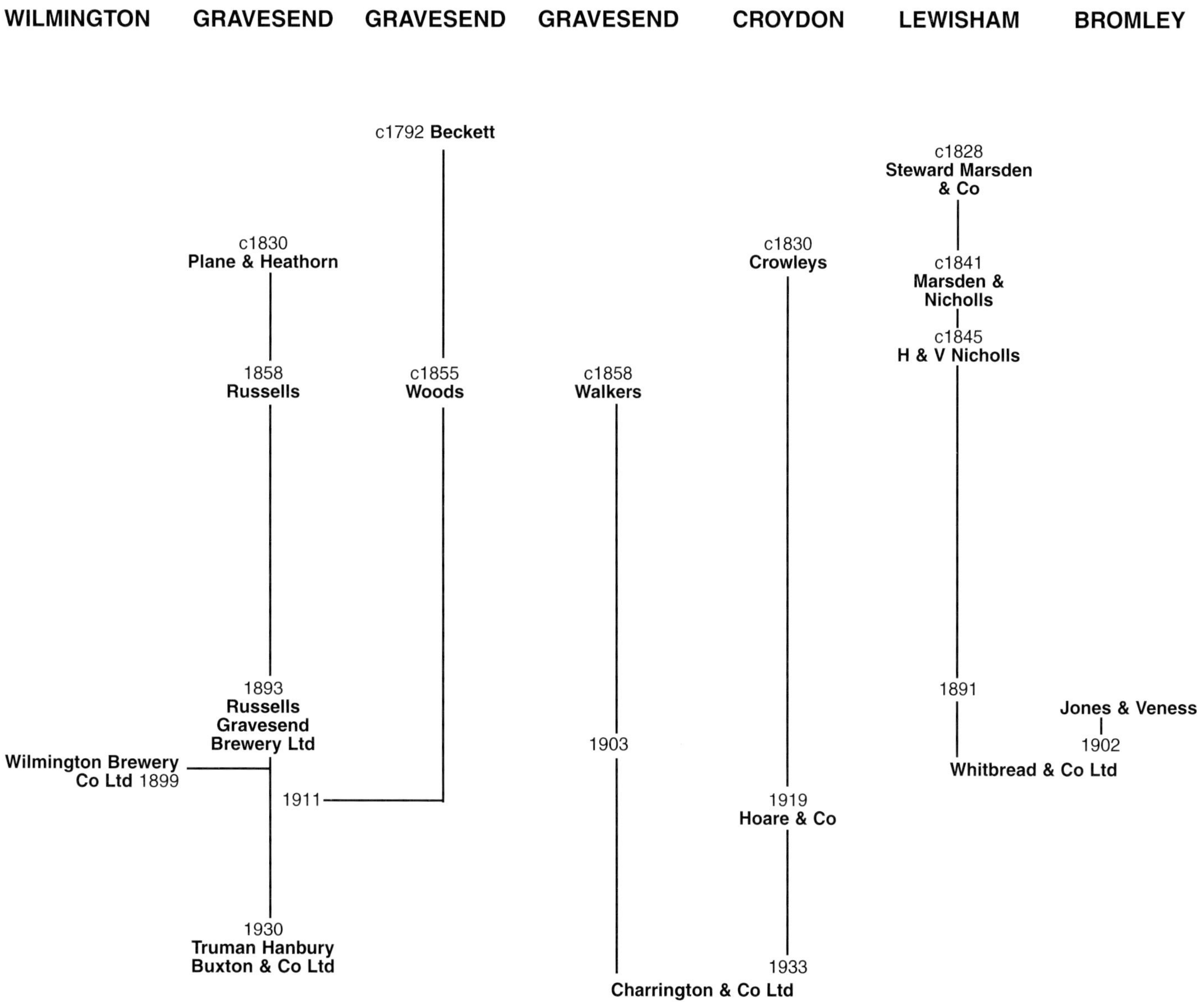

WILMINGTON	GRAVESEND	GRAVESEND	GRAVESEND	CROYDON	LEWISHAM	BROMLEY

c1792 **Beckett**

c1828
**Steward Marsden
& Co**

c1830
Plane & Heathorn

c1830
Crowleys

c1841
**Marsden &
Nicholls**

c1845
H & V Nicholls

1858
Russells

c1855
Woods

c1858
Walkers

1891

Jones & Veness

1893
**Russells
Gravesend
Brewery Ltd**

1902

**Wilmington Brewery
Co Ltd** 1899

1903

Whitbread & Co Ltd

1911

1919
Hoare & Co

1930
**Truman Hanbury
Buxton & Co Ltd**

1933

Charrington & Co Ltd

The Seven Stars, Footscray, c.1910

Appendix V

Postscript

Postscript 1

*N*ot everything is cut and dried; there is still much to learn about the early history of our pubs. Whilst I had concentrated on pubs up until 1918, for the purposes of this book I needed to discover basic facts about some of our modern pubs or their rebuilds. It was most surprising how elusive some facts were.

I accept responsibility for any errors which may have crept in (though I would blame someone else if I could!) or claim that the beer was off and I couldn't think straight.

I hope this book will raise questions that others of you may be able to answer or to provide photos, documents or memories which will increase the knowledge of for me, this exciting part of our local history.

Postscript 2 - A cautionary tale

*W*hilst this book may end up being used for pub quizzes do not let it provoke anything other than friendly argument. After an entry in 1880 in the Burial Registers for North Cray is a note; 'buried by coroners order' and 'killed at the Seven Stars Inn Footscray by one Wells'.

John Wells was drinking in the pub with his brother Fred against whom a rumour was alleged to have been circulated by a Joseph Francis that Fred owed their employer, local farmer and faggot merchant Mr Attree, £16. Francis that fateful night left his home a short walk away and entered the Seven Stars for a jug of beer to take home for supper and had a pint while he was there. John Wells saw him and confronted him about the rumour and then hit him, knocking Francis's head through a pane of glass. He then retired back to his brother and paid the landlord 8d for the damage he had caused. Still simmering Wells returned and this time gave Francis two heavy blows to the head which caused him to collapse. He dragged Francis outside. Mrs Francis, wondering why her husband had not returned, came looking and discovered her husband dead.

The moral of the story is do not get into arguments, the outcome of which you cannot predict.

Postscript 3 - One for the Road

I hope this work will encourage you to try other pubs in the London Borough of Bexley, to see if their history still imparts some ambience. However if you travel by your own transport be a responsible and not an anti-social dangerous citizen and therefore DO NOT drink and drive.

Index